train wreck

**The true story behind
the Silver Spring, Maryland
commuter rail disaster**

Tom Low

The Spartina Press

This is a work of NONFICTION. All the people in it are identified by their real names. Every word of dialogue has a documented source in either taped interviews by the author or depositions and public hearings conducted by the U.S. National Transportation Safety Board.

CSX Transportation Inc. dispatcher conversations were recorded by that company on their audio system located in Jacksonville, Florida, and later transcribed into print for federal investigators. Quotes from those transcriptions are shown in a smaller font.

Nothing in this narrative was fabricated.

It Began as an Ordinary Day in February

Don Noble, a 49-year-old veteran engineer who has been operating trains for almost twenty years, gently rolls his two huge locomotives and fifteen trailing cars past the small Silver Spring, Maryland, station. It is not a scheduled station stop. He is operating the daily Amtrak *Capitol Limited* bound for Pittsburgh and Chicago and loaded with passengers, baggage and mail, the usual Friday afternoon mix.

Because heavy snow has been clogging a switch along its path near the Washington D.C. terminal yard, one of the CSX Railroad Company's dispatchers down in Jacksonville, Florida, has temporarily routed Noble's train onto the inbound set of tracks instead of the parallel outbound ones and restricted its speed. That is normal. No big deal. The dispatchers often use this common maneuver up and down their lines when they need to move a train around problems such as a broken-down freight or tracks under repair.

Rumbling into a right-to-left curve, Noble and his young assistant engineer, Joey Fratangelo, see the lights up on the tall trackside-mast to their right. It is showing a "medium clear" signal with two illuminated green bulbs and a single white one below. That means that the dispatcher has set the upcoming switch at Georgetown Junction to send the Amtrak over to the normal outbound tracks. Noble advances his throttle from notch 3 to 4 as he comes out of the bend. The 16th Street Bridge above him frames the gray afternoon sky and vacant straightaway ahead. Once his train has passed through the crossover, Noble can increase his speed from 30 to 79 miles an hour and start making time up the Potomac River Valley through Western Maryland.

He looks up from the gauges on his control stand and out through the front windshield. Between the sideways whacks of the windshield wipers, Noble's eyes lock on something about a half mile up the tracks, something that doesn't seem right. It appears to be the headlamp of a train coming out of the distant curve on his track, and it is moving fast.

In fact, it is the P286, a Maryland Area Rail Commuter (MARC) train on its normal afternoon trip from Brunswick, Maryland into the nation's capital. Engineer Ricky Orr is driving the three passenger coaches from inside a small compartment in the front car with a single locomotive pushing them from the rear. A group of high-school-age students, many of whom are sleeping, have spread themselves throughout the long passenger compartment directly behind him.

The train's two conductors, Jimmy Major and Jim Quillen stand beside Orr in the engineer's cab, visiting with him. After a long day, they are running only a couple of minutes behind schedule. The MARC train races through the blowing snow at 65 miles per hour as it passes under the Brookville Road Bridge. A high bank on its left obscures any view of the upcoming Georgetown Junction signals 500 yards ahead. Only when they reach the end of the long curve will Orr, Major and Quillen be able to see them. The three men are most likely talking and certainly not anticipating anything unusual.

And then, *what in the hell is that up ahead?* - RED, stop lights on the distant signal towers? And beyond that, the headlight of a train moving out of the curve toward them? Orr and the conductors struggle to rationalize the scene ahead. Is the train on their track or the parallel one over to their left? Is it slowing down? Orr knocks his throttle down four notches. Critical seconds click off the clock.

Damian Benetiz, one of the students standing in the aisle of the coach looks through the open interior-door to the engineer's compartment and sees one of the conductors jerk his head forward, appear to look intently at something, rock backward and then lean into the windshield again.

Engineer Orr snaps out of his moment of disbelief. The oncoming train *is* on *his* track and does not appear to be slowing down. Grabbing his air-brake handle, he jerks it over to the emergency position. His three seconds of hesitation, however, have consumed almost 300 additional feet of track. The air-brake reservoirs on his three cars and engine release their stored power slamming brake shoes against train wheels. Without any warning, the student passengers are suddenly jerked forward.

The two conductors, concerned about their young charges, bolt through the open door behind them into the passenger compartment. Jimmy Major is in the lead. He and Jim Quillen grab the seat backs hand over hand and pull themselves through the car. With the train powering down, it is like trying to climb up a steep hill. Both are screaming the same warning, "Move to the back! Get down! Brace yourselves!"

Amtrak Engineer Don Noble calls over to his assistant engineer without looking at him. "Joey, look at this son-of-a-bitch! We have the green signal, he's got the red!"

Joey rises out of his seat, slides across the cab floor behind his engineer, slowly opens the door and steps outside onto the cold metal ladder. Noble is too distracted to miss him.

3

One

Willis Henry was one of the few black conductors working on the Baltimore and Washington area MARC commuter trains. Soft-spoken and looking much younger than his 44 years, Henry, like everyone else around him in passenger service, had plodded his way up the slow and regimented career path that had been strictly maintained by the railroads for over a hundred years.

If he had known when hired on with the Baltimore and Ohio (B&O) in 1971 that it would be 25 years before he could get a regular position with predictable hours, he probably would have quit on the spot. But he kept his head down and stuck it out. At one point, after thirteen years, he was laid off for several months as a switchman and went to work for the U.S. Postal Service.

A few months later the B&O called him back and made him a freight conductor. While that seemed like a nice promotion, he was still working temporary, "extra board" assignments. The extra board is a list of men who remain available 24 hours a day, seven days a week, to fill the jobs of senior crew members who have taken leave or are otherwise unavailable for their regular runs.

In 1986, Henry got another break, of sorts. The company phoned his house and asked him if he wanted to work a temporary assignment as a passenger train conductor. The job was on a MARC commuter that left Baltimore at 4 p.m., traveled to Washington and returned at 8. It was four hours work, but he would receive a full day's pay. That was all it took to sell him on passenger service.

Over the next nine years, extra-board duty yielded him only about 160 days of work a year, but he finally acquired enough time and reputation to grab what he really wanted, a "regular" passenger-train conductor's position. Beginning on January 1, 1996, he reported to the Baltimore Riverside Yard every weekday at 10 in the morning. From there, he and a senior conductor, Jim Quillen, and Engineer Ricky Orr, picked up and ran a late-morning commuters along a forty-mile route into Union Station in Washington. Early in the afternoon they made another trip fifty miles west to the own of Brunswick.

At 4:30 p.m. the three men took almost empty MARC express back into Washington. The final leg of their daily journey was operating the last commuter train from there to Baltimore. They didn't wrap up until after 10 at night. Henry was away from home for twelve hours a day, but he was delighted with what he had achieved.

In late January, 1995, he decided to take several days' leave and drive his mother down to Newport News, Virginia, and up to New Jersey and Philadelphia to see her three sisters. During the trip, the clutch on his 1992 Ford Taurus began to stick. Over the next week it continued to deteriorate. He knew that he had to get it fixed because his son used the car every weekday to attend a private high school in Baltimore. A trip to the garage, however, would require him to "mark-off" an entire day of work. He kept putting off the inevitable, but by the first week in February, the clutch was barely engaging.

Henry finally approached his supervisor, Jim Gray, and asked him for a day off. Gray gave him a choice of Monday, the 12th of February, or Friday the 16th. Henry chose Friday.

That month, Jimmy Major, a passenger conductor with high seniority, was working as a freight-switching foreman in the Baltimore yards. He transferred into that position because he needed an eight-hour, daytime shift close to home while his wife, Peggy, was recovering from surgery. At the same time, Major had kept his name on the railroad's extra list for passenger operations so he would not lose his standing in road service. At 10 at night on Thursday, the 15th of February, Peggy answered the phone at their home. The company caller told her that her husband was to fill-in for Henry on a MARC commuter train the next morning.

When Willis Henry arrived at the dealership for his car appointment, he was pleasantly surprised to find that it was still under the mileage warranty. "I felt blessed," he later said. Since the repair work would take several hours, he walked across the street through a driving snowstorm, found a comfortable wing-chair in a Borders bookstore and started reading a magazine. It wasn't until after he had picked up the car, driven home and turned on his television that he heard the news. The MARC train that he should have been on that day had been involved in a terrible accident.

Back at work the following Tuesday morning, everyone around the office called him "the luckiest conductor that ever lived." By that time, however, Henry knew what had happened to the crew and the kids. He told them, "Sorry, fellows, but I don't look at it that way."

Two

Friday, February 16, 1996
Morning

At 3:45 a.m., the National Weather Service's office in Sterling, Virginia, northwest of Washington, D.C., issued the following weather forecast:

Winter storm warning; snow is expected across the Washington and Baltimore metropolitan areas today with accumulations of 3 to 6 inches. Temperatures will be in the lower 30s. Northeasterly winds are currently 10 to 15 miles per hour and will rise to 25 miles per hour and remain gusty this afternoon.

Conductor Jim Quillen walked out of his house on the outskirts of Frederick, Maryland at 8:30, climbed into his car and began his 45 mile drive east on Interstate 70 to the Baltimore beltway. There he merged into the traffic-clogged southbound lanes. At 9:15, Engineer Ricky Orr pulled away from his home in the Baltimore suburb of Glen Burnie and continued north and east toward the big downtown.

Within a mile of the city's Inner Harbor and high-tech skyline, each of them exited the elevated I-95 expressway and dropped down a ramp into the bleak industrial landscape below. There they paused at a traffic light beneath the concrete interstate, turned left and made their ways out of the shadows up Key Street back into the sunlight.

At the top of the hill, the railroad men found East Fort Avenue, a residential street that eventually passed through part of the Locust Point Marine Terminal and ended on the grounds of Ft. McHenry – the citadel that inspired Marylander Francis Scott Key to write *The Star Spangled Banner* almost 200 years earlier.

Instead of continuing down those eight blocks, they made an immediate right beside the Southside Market Plaza and drove around behind it into the CSX Railroad Company's Riverside Yard.

At that point in time Riverside Yard was a sad remainder of its former self. Ninety years earlier it had been the proud site of the Baltimore and Ohio Railroad Company's premiere engine and car maintenance shops. The twin roundhouses, built in 1907 with 50 stalls for steam engines, had been demolished in the 1950s, and all that remained in 1996 were three small brick buildings, a large metal-sided one and an outdoor turntable where a few men could still turn locomotives around or work beneath them. The small complex was then being operated by CSX to service and store the State of Maryland MARC commuter trains.

Within a few minutes of each other, Ricky Orr and Jim Quillen parked their cars in the bleak, concrete lot, steeled themselves against the cold wind and walked into the small, brick crew-office. There they were surprised to find Willis Henry's replacement for the day, their old friend Jimmy Major. Orr and Quillen had known Major for over twenty years, but his recent job assignments had taken him off in different directions. It was a happy, hand-shaking reunion for the three of them.

Orr picked up their printed train-orders while the two conductors began inspecting the three, metal-silver, blue-and-orange-striped passenger coaches. At 10:40 Orr moved their train a half-mile up the tracks onto the main line and into the center of the old port city. The ancient, seven-story B&O warehouse towered against the gray sky over to their left for the last quarter mile down the dead-end track. Since 1905, this warehouse has remained the longest building on the East Coast of the United States. In its prime, it could hold a thousand boxcar loads of merchandise.

In 1992, the brick backside of this enormous structure began its new function as a dramatic backdrop to one of the masterpieces of modern urban architecture, Oriole Park at Camden Yards. That year, William Donald Schaefer, the innovative four-term Mayor of Baltimore and two-term governor of Maryland, dedicated a new standard for major league baseball stadiums, a spectacular and breathtaking amphitheater dramatically crafted into the towering cityscape only two blocks from Babe Ruth's birthplace.

The MARC train eased to a stop behind another visually striking building, the historic three-story Camden Station. The passenger function of this Civil-War-period, Italianate-style terminal had long been relocated outside into an insignificant hut in its back parking lot. The nearby, plain and uncovered platform was the spot where conductors Quillen and Major would load the first passengers for their routine day's journey.

Their commuter train was designated the P251 ("P" stood for passenger). Its running weight was a relatively light 270 tons, and its length, 279 feet, could fit onto a football field with yards to spare. The crew was set to make four separate runs over the course of the next eleven and one-half hours - Baltimore into Washington, Washington to Brunswick, back to Washington and out to Baltimore.

That late in the morning there were only six regular stops on their Camden Line into the nation's capital and few riders. It was also the Friday preceding the Presidents Day holiday weekend (Monday off) and the weather was dreadful. Many of their regular customers had just stayed home.

The normal one-hour trip into Washington was delayed, however. Snow and ice had jammed switches along the route and railroad maintenance crews were scrambling to dig them out. The MARC crew finally docked their train at the city's Union Station at 12:59, forty-nine minutes late.

Jim Quillen walked across the rear concourse to the terminal crew office to pick up the train orders for the next leg of their trip, while Jimmy Major ducked into the food court to grab some hot coffee for his buddies.

Three

The people who turn out to be naturals in railroad jobs are those who learn fast, require minimal supervision and quickly become effective members of a team. When a man reached the point where he could make all the right moves in the right order with seamless perfection, those around him would say that he had "swing." Back when passenger trains had full-service dining cars, that word defined the nimble waiter in the starched white uniform spiriting trays piled high with hot food and beverages down the aisle of a rocking dining car without spilling a morsel.

James E. Major, Jr., Richard W. Orr, James Quillen and their colleague Russell Bly all honed their swing over many years.. The four of them began their railroad careers working together in the late 1960s and the early 1970s as "ground men" (brakemen and switchmen) for the B&O in Baltimore.

If the four were standing against a wall by height, the line would start with Major. He was the smallest at 5' 5" and carried less than 140 pounds. Jimmy was part of an old and extended railroad family. His sister, Anna, worked as a ticket agent on the Camden MARC commuter line. His brother, George, was an East End (Baltimore) brakeman, and his grandfather had been a West End engineer.

He and his wife, Peggy, had known each other since they were eleven years old in the fifth grade, The Majors lived in a residential part of Linthicum, a community not far from the Baltimore-Washington International Airport. Throughout the neighborhood he was known as "Mr. Jimmy, the Mayor of Linthicum Lane." Some on the railroad said he looked like a bulldog that would rather bite you than meet you, but with just a little face to face conversation, he could quickly become your good friend.

Ricky Orr, another Baltimore-area native, was slightly taller but weighed less. Youthful and wiry with curly hair flowing to his shoulders, his trim and drooping mustache brought to mind Robert Redford playing the Sundance Kid. Twinkling eyes and a charming wit drew people from across a room to talk with him.

At 5' 11" and 175 pounds, Russell Bly would later sport a signature belly between bright red suspenders. "Captain Bly" was also from a railroad family but had been raised a country boy in the rural area west of Baltimore and lived in an old Victorian house on the main street of Mt. Airy village. Russell's trademarks were an easy demeanor and optimistic outlook that never wavered. He could make blue, four-letter words sound like poetry and extract a morsel of street wisdom or humor from any crisis, quandary or quagmire.

At the end of the line would be Jim Quillen with his aviator, tear-drop glasses. His most distinguishing physical feature was the "bishop-style," hedge of hair that ringed his bald dome. A rock-solid, 180-pound frame made him appear physically imposing, but that impression was quickly offset when he started talking. A slow, rambling squeaky voice coupled with the fact that he often had to think for more than a few seconds before he answered a question made a listener anxious to coax the words out of him. A strict guy that worked by the book, he was not a man inclined to chat with someone he didn't know.

Quillen lived in the southeast Baltimore community of Brooklyn. Separated from downtown by a bridge spanning the Patapsco River, this four-square-mile town was built on a peninsula that once prided itself as a summer gambling retreat for inner city dwellers. By the 1990s it had evolved into a quiet residential enclave of 23,000 souls living on tree-lined streets in tidy, single-family houses, apartments and townhouses. Generous parks with grassy baseball fields sheltered their homes from the neighborhood bars that lined the main drag. It was the place where you might find Baltimore's Democrat version of Archie and Edith Bunker.

For railroaders, Brooklyn had always been an ideal place to live because, a man, if he wanted the exercise, could virtually walk from his home to the nearby Curtis Bay rail yard. The B&O rotated its new recruits through all of their yards around the greater metropolitan area, and Curtis Bay (at the southern entrance into the Harbor Tunnel today) was the largest. It had never been anything more than a vast, treeless plain bordering an inland reach of the Chesapeake Bay with miles of parallel railroad tracks, parked freight cars, elevated coal pier, a half mile of water-side coal shoots, gigantic liquid-storage tanks and mountains of loose minerals piled on the ground. This is where the B&O brought those raw materials to load onto ships.

Orr, Major and Bly started working there when they were older teens, and all they could get was the midnight, 12 p.m. to 8 a.m. shift (popularly known as the "third trick"). Claiming a position in one of the other eight-hour time slots, daylight (first trick) or matinee, was out of the question for years. They could, however, simply show up for switching work six or seven days a week and make good money.

Jim Quillen was slightly older than the other three and had been working the yard for a couple of years when the new boys arrived. In spite of their inexperience, Jim chose to adopt them. In turn, they grew to respect him as a mentor and even began calling him "Mother." Whenever the chicks got confused about how to handle a switching maneuver, Quillen would show them the way. In time, they proudly anointed themselves as, "The Crew."

One of their daily jobs was "cutting up" long freights and recombining their cars into new trains bound for different locations, or sets that would be emptied on the site. This two-fold process was called classification, and The Crew did it by "working the hump" and "flat switching."

Working the hump required an engineer to shove (push) a freight train from the rear up onto an artificial elevation - a small man-made hill. The brakemen/switchmen, set the switches, disconnected cars according to a written plan and let them roll down the other side of the incline into one of many holding tracks. Major, Quillen, Bly and Orr would take turns riding a loose group of them while struggling to twist one or more of the cars' rusting handbrakes closed.

If the set of cars was longer than six, the brakeman would "tie down" the first brake, jump off the car, wait a second, catch the grab bar of another one, swing up onto it and continue the manual braking process until the cars were brought to a stop. These maneuvers were especially difficult when snow and biting winds swirled off of the open-water harbor and built up inches of ice along the rails.

The yards were not lighted at night, so each man carried a battery-powered lantern to find his way. Climbing down off his cars in the dark, he had to remain alert since another ten might be silently rolling down the tracks a few feet behind him. He could see the silhouettes of box and tank cars with his lantern, but the beam would often miss or overshoot the occasional line of empty flat ones. Their thin profiles made them invisible killers.

Once the brakeman had secured hand brakes on sets of cars dead-ended into a holding track, he would walk up or down the line to make sure that the coupler knuckle on the last car was open. If its receiving coupler was shut, the next oncoming group of cars would bounce off it. The man then had to open the thing so that the next cut would ram the two knuckles closed and locked. BAM!

One night Russell Bly opened a jammed single knuckle and stepped up on top of it just as another four cars came out of the dark and plowed into the coupler. He was only slightly shaken, but when he climbed down onto the ground, Bly found that he was also off balance. Both the heels on his heavy-duty work boots had been sheared off. It could have been his feet.

The second method The Crew used to cut and recombine trains was flat switching. In the early 1970s, that required the services of five men. The engineer sat in the time honored spot on the right side of the locomotive cab. The fireman took his position on the left. The three other men worked on the ground. If the train was being shoved, the conductor would station himself within ten car-lengths of the locomotive so that the engineer or fireman could see him. A flagman stood down the line, as far as he could get within the sight of the conductor. The brakeman was further back, but in a position where could see the flagman. The flagman's jobs were to relay information forward or rearward and open the couplers linking the cars at those points where the cuts were to be made.

The crew disconnected the air-brake hoses between the cars before they started "the move." Since they most often operated beyond the earshot of one another and did not have two-way radios, all of them used hand signals in daylight and flares after dark. When a man would go out of sight because of a curve or a building, the rest of them had to estimate how long he would be blocked and remain prepared to stop the train when he was gone for more time than that.

If a switching crew had a freight train with forty cars and orders to cut it into eight sets using flat switching, each one had to be disconnected from the train and rolled onto its own holding track. The crew would first review the action plan and then take their places while the engineer started moving the train backward. The brakemen, flagman and conductor on the ground fast walked, almost jogged, alongside it. At a certain point, the flagman jerked the coupler open and sent a signal to the head-end brakeman that he had done so. That man notified the engineer.

The engineer then applied his engine brake to let the disconnected set roll away from the rest of the train. The brakeman running ahead would open a switch to route the disconnected cars onto the holding track. As the cars clicked past him at 20 miles per hour, he would seize a grab-bar on the side of one of them, pull himself up onto the steel ladder, make his way to the brake wheel and begin turning it to slow the cars.

At the same time, one of the other men would close the switch to keep the balance of the train advancing up the main feeder line. The process would be replicated seven more times. If everyone correctly anticipated each move, the engineer could keep his train rolling while the ground men cut off blocks of cars like clockwork.

That maneuver was called "switching cuts on the fly" and represented a dangerous source of pride for railroad men working on their swing. If a brakeman needed the engineer to slow down to a normal walking pace for him, they'd call him a cripple. The yard supervisors loved that kind of action and ignored its safety implications.

Even though The Crew was working in the dark, they soon saw the light and figured out how to game the system. The old school of railroading was all about working for a "quit" or a "back-off." The company in those days paid them to finish a daily assigned set of tasks and didn't care if the men were out there for six hours or twelve as long as they got the jobs done.

That led Bly, Major, Quillen and Orr - college material that never attended a class - to start thinking in terms of macro strategy, like they were playing a game of chess or checkers. How could they accomplish their work using the least number of switching moves? Since their goal was to get done and go home, they began questioning the labor-intensive instructions issued by the senior yard men, or de facto line supervisors. They were highly skilled, but their numbers contained many who could barely read or write. That meant they were only comfortable with receiving and giving verbal instructions. To overcome this lack of formal education, they perfected the art of memorizing complex lists of tasks. After visiting the tower and talking privately with the yardmaster, they would come back down to the tracks without written orders in hand and start barking out assignments to their "subordinates."

We're going down to track number ten, knock-off (release) that train's brakes, move it up and make 16 cuts. I'll tell you what to do next when the time comes.

Believing that they were definitely smarter and certainly more efficient, The Crew began firing back comments like - *Why are we doing it that way? We want to see the orders. You have 48 cars on that track, and you got us making 16 cuts. Why that many cuts? Let's pull the whole 48 cars out and start dropping them "in" using a logical plan rather than a piecemeal approach.*

The rookies, however, did admire one unique skill that some of the older men had refined over their 30 to 40 years. Periodically, the yardmaster would call up and dispatch one of the experienced switchmen or conductors down to bring him back a full report listing the recently arrived freights that were out there and how they were lined up. The guy would stand alongside the rails without pencil or paper and watch while "the man" ran a one-hundred-and-two car freight past him. The switchman or conductor would then walk back to the office and write down the composition of the entire train; the identification numbers (two to four letters and up to six digits) from every car, its position in the line and whether it was a loader or an empty.

Jimmy Major soon became one of the talented switchmen; his mind operated like a human camera. After only a couple years on the job, he prided himself in being able to read ten pages of instructions in the morning and then give his buddies the daily "skinny" about the cars that needed to be cut and combined all day without ever referring back to the written text. A historical footnote: the barcode was first adopted by the nations' railroads (not supermarkets) to electronically read and record the identity of freight cars.

By the early-1970s, Russ Bly began to feel that yard work was going stale for him. The railroad had started cracking down on unsafe practices - such as jumping onto and off moving trains. Crews were also no longer allowed to speed up their assigned chores and complete them in less than 8 hours. To make things worse, inspectors began skulking around the yard buildings and hiding "in the weeds" with video cameras trying catch those who weren't falling in line. For the railroaders, all the challenge and fun had been taken out of their work.

Then one day in 1973, the company approached the four members of The Crew with a blanket invitation to enter engineer training. Ricky Orr was the only taker. Bly seriously considered it because his father and uncle were both active engineers. He took several days off and rode with both of them on their jobs. After a week, however, he found it boring.

"I realized that I didn't want to spend the next 30 years sitting in the same seat all day with my head hanging out the window of an engine cab taking crap from conductors and brakemen on the ground," he said.

Instead, he decided to sign up for the freewheeling, freight-switching jobs still available along the old main line that ran directly west from Baltimore and skirted his hometown of Mt. Airy on its way to Brunswick. At Harpers Ferry, a branch extended down into the Shenandoah Valley of Virginia. The men along those routes could still do their work the way they wanted. Plus, the company paid "road switchers" a little extra money. Bly tried to convince Quillen and Major to come with him, but they shook their heads and stayed in the Baltimore yards.

One wintry night in his new role, Bly found himself spotting freight cars (aligning them to a warehouse platform) with a small crew at the Mt. Airy Cold Storage facility. The men were using two engines to pull their load up the steep Parr's Ridge off of the main to a single-track siding at the top of the hill. To save time, they decided to split the motors (engines). The brakeman would cut one of them off the delivery train, and the engineer and he would run it to the front of the warehouse to pick up the empties that were parked there.

Bly's assignment was to open the gate on the tracks leading to the rear of the warehouse, set the switch, climb onto the second locomotive and use it to shove the loaded cars that they had brought with them back up alongside the loading dock.

After he had disconnected and tied-down those cars, he could run his single engine back out, close the gate and reset the switch so that the engineer and brakeman coming down the other side of the building with their engine pulling the empties could connect to him. At that point, the crew could run back to the main yard, call it a day and go home. All in all, it appeared to be a well conceived plan.

Then thread by thread, it became unraveled. After he set the switch and before he climbed aboard his locomotive, Bly had a sudden urge to take a pee. Standing on the ground in the winter wind with his fly open, he cursed when it blew his hat off. He chased the thing through the snow for a couple of yards, but just as he reached down to grab it, his heart sank. The whistle in the engine cab behind him gave a faint toot. That meant the air brakes were starting to re-charge and release. Slowly, very slowly, the train began drifting backward down Parr's Ridge.

"I'm running like hell through a foot of snow," he remembered, "Got as close as a couple of inches to the grab-bar and couldn't get a-hold of it, couldn't get on the locomotive. So I just stood there bended over with my hands on my knees, breathing hard and watching an engine, caboose and four freezer-cars full of French fries move off into the night by themselves."

He later found out that the train had accelerated to 77 miles per hour over eight miles before it left the rails on a curve near Reel's Mill.

The next day the company fired the entire crew.

Bly languished at home for over six months. Then one evening he happened to strike up a conversation with a distant personal acquaintance, who, as it turned out, was a friend of the railroad's president. Within a week, the hapless Mt. Airy Cold Storage crew was back on the job.

That was fine, Bly had salvaged his job, but over the coming year he began to notice strange changes creeping into the work. The conductors he was reporting to appeared to be half his age, and it seemed like the company was hiring them off the street one day and promoting them the next. After months of training the new "kids" how to supervise *him,* Bly knew what he had to do. He held his nose, closed his eyes and jumped into conductor training.

His friends, Quillen and Major, thought he had lost his mind. With over 11 years seniority, all three of them were finally enjoying regular daylight schedules. They knew that Bly was going to face what every railroader dreaded when he changed job categories; a career switch to conductor would wipe out a decade of seniority earned as a brakeman and drop him to the bottom of another long ranking list. As a new freight conductor, Bly winced when he got his starting number - 833.

When a freshman conductor completed his training, he was required to establish, and follow, his turn. The word "turn" is as old as the railroad itself and only applies to engineers and conductors in road, not yard, service. It seems to be a composite of several similar notions; a place in line (your turn), a specific train run (the P251 is a turn), a round trip (turnaround run) and even "turning over" a train to a new crew. The Baltimore Division, for example, had some 40 conductor turns in passenger service. That meant there were 40 regular jobs for passenger train conductors.

A trainee freight or passenger conductor established his turn in the Baltimore West-End territory by riding three round trips between that city, Washington and Brunswick with a road foreman. He could then "mark up" (officially make himself available) for jobs in his new position. Both the company and the union set that date as the official starting point of his seniority in road service, and it remained anchored in his record, unchanged for the rest of the man's career. The same rule applied to engineers.

Russell Bly's decision to start over in a different job proved to be a prophetic one. In 1981, just a few years after he made the move to conductor, the railroad began phasing out large numbers of yard jobs and sandbagging all the high-seniority brakemen by declaring that they would all be required to become conductors over the next four years. Since he had moved early, Bly was catapulted up the growing list of freshly-minted conductors cramming in behind him.

Jim Quillen and Jimmy Major attended the required conductor-training sessions but held out against the possibility of relocating and continued to work switching jobs in Baltimore. In 1992, the company again shocked the remaining yard workers by telling them that everyone had to establish a road turn. For Quillen and Major, that meant that they were finally forced to leave the yard and go out on the road as junior conductors, subordinate to others who had substantially less total service time than they did.

Jimmy Major held onto his job in the Baltimore yards, but Jim Quillen gave that up and began riding freights out to Western Maryland. According to Russ Bly, "Quillen had become stressed out by the yard and at the same time found himself in-between families. For some reason he couldn't hold onto a wife for very long."

Quillen's problems were a common occupational hazard in the railroad business. Over time, however, he found a great woman (Betty) and the two of them decided to leave their home in Brooklyn and buy a house out in the country near Frederick. There they could also find good health care for his son. While Jim didn't miss the hassle of the Baltimore yards, Betty continued to long for the city life.

Some described Quillen's general spirit and demeanor as "laid back," but that was a deceiving facade. He had twice been cited by the company for outstanding, heroic actions in Baltimore.

Local residents would occasionally walk across the sea of tracks at the Curtis Bay complex. One day, a woman pushing a baby in a stroller through the yard somehow got its wheels stuck in an open switch. Quillen was riding on the head end of a train bearing down on them and could see her panicked attempts to un-strap the child from the contraption. He jumped off the locomotive, sprinted down the tracks ahead of it and pulled the baby out of the carriage just before the engine crushed it. Even though the train was moving at only 20 miles per hour, the engineer couldn't have stopped it in time.

In the second episode, a ten-year-old girl had found her way out into the yard and stepped into a power switch just as the tower operator closed it. The switch crushed her foot. Quillen, who was working on a nearby freight, saw her tragic plight and raced across sixty yards of intervening tracks, pulled off his belt and wrapped it around the girl's leg to keep her from bleeding to death. Then he ran to the tower to call an ambulance. They didn't have portable radios or 911 back then. The little girl lived but lost part of her foot.

Jimmy Major, on the other hand, was the one member of The Crew that found his passion in labor activities. According to his wife Peggy, that began in 1988 as the result of an injury. One afternoon he was on top of a freight car tying down a hand brake when the engineer released the train's air brakes. That jerked the cars forward and threw Major off and down onto an adjoining set of tracks. With a shattered foot, he lay unconscious across the rails for about a minute before waking up and rolling out of the way of an oncoming freight.

After several operations, three-and-one-half years of rehab and recovery, he returned to work with one leg shorter than the other and a couple of steel pins in his heel. During his recuperation, he accepted a position in the union's office working on pending claims cases. That was called committee work, and the railroad companies often gave their employees paid leaves-of-absences (according to the union contract) to do it.

Later he served for a brief period as the secretary for Local 610 of the United Transportation Union (UTU) in the Baltimore Division. Major's heart-felt concern for the average worker and his outspoken nature, however, led him to start questioning what he called the local's "time-worn" mode of operation. The members of The Crew, for example, were all West-End boys and their local president, an East-End man, appeared to be constantly coddling the complainers and slackers in his old district. That ran against Major's grain. The railroad company really, on the other hand, really didn't care; they let the unions play their games as long as overall production remained up to standards.

Major began trying to change the UTU, and the union's entrenched senior officers encouraged him to leave. He considered becoming a company trainmaster and work against the union from the company side, but after some thought, couldn't convince himself to support the railroad's labor practices. After a long period of inactivity, he finally reunited with the union and became a topnotch representative and local chairman.

As Major, Quillen and Bly entered their forties, each of them began to realize that their knees and youthful stamina were giving out. The years of "beating the ballast" – running up and down the tracks on gravel – had taken their toll. They also no longer woke up in the morning ready to hit the ground running, especially when the weather outside was harsh.

Bly was actively searching for his next move, and that sent him to his father. Dad offered him one piece of advice. "Son," he said, "There are a lot of bull shitters out there on the railroad. What *you* need to do is find out which man is making the most money. That's the guy who knows what he is doing, the most qualified one on his way up. You watch him, work with him and learn his tricks."

Bly followed his suggestion and began shadowing the highest-paid conductor working the road out of Brunswick, the legendary Leechel Reynolds. When his man moved from freights to passenger trains, Bly made some inquiries and discovered that passenger service offered the same money for an eight-hour shift that he was taking home after twelve hours in freight.

That, he learned, was because the pay for conductors and engineers working in passenger service was based on the number of miles they traveled each day, not how long they were on the job. In 1982 a day's work was 100 miles. By 1996, the distance had been increased to 130 miles. Today it is even higher. If a man's run was two sets of roundtrips over the course of a day and totaled at least 260 miles, he was paid twice the daily wage. The conductors were also decked out in spiffy uniforms and comfortable shoes and spent their hours in air-conditioned or heated coaches with the passengers.

Not all the conductors, however, aspired to move into passenger service. Yard-switching jobs were predictable eight-hour days with every weekend off. An engineer or conductor who worked there returned home by 5 or 6 p.m. and got to know his kids.

In contrast, most of the passenger jobs were scheduled with long periods of down time between each leg of their trips. Many conductors and engineers working on trains into Washington arrived at Union Station early in the morning and departed late in the afternoon. Those were the low seniority, turns that everyone had spent some time in, but no one would actually bid on. During the day the men were stuck in the city and spent their time sitting or sleeping in cheap hotels. Alcoholism and infidelity became lurking demons that ruined many of their marriages. Most adapted well and stuck it out, realizing that the long-term monetary advantages outweighed the potential pitfalls. A few resourceful men kept automobiles near the city and drove home and back during the day.

Russell Bly again took the lead and decided to move into passenger service. His friends Jimmy Major and Jim Quillen eventually got the message and followed him. Major didn't need much convincing after his injury; passenger work was definitely safer. The fact that he and Quillen had dallied over the years and lost seniority in the periods of sweeping railroad-company changes would play a pivotal role on the day of the coming accident.

Four

Railroad men who were looking for a little more thrill in their jobs became engineers. They were the few who wanted to run the show alone, controlling 10,000 tons of rolling stock moving at 80 miles-per-hour and wondering what was waiting around the next curve.

After only two years working as a brakeman, Ricky Orr could not wait to get into the cab of a locomotive. Unlike Major, Quillen and Bly, he grabbed the company's offer to enter engineer training in 1973. It was an amazing opportunity for a nineteen year old. Almost all of his predecessors in that field came from the ranks of older locomotive firemen who labored 20 years waiting for a chance to move over into the engineer's seat.

The seeds of an engineer shortage had been sowed years earlier (in the mid 1960s) by the Baltimore and Ohio Railroad Company when it launched a massive campaign to retire firemen. Except for trains operating very long distances, or those carrying dangerous cargos, diesel locomotives required the service of only one man in the cab.

In 1972, the Chessie System acquired a controlling interest in the B&O, quickly discovered that it had been handed a severely depleted stock of future engineers (firemen), and set

CSX

about to remedy that problem by establishing several fast-track apprentice-engineer schools.

One of the programs was located in the old Western Maryland City of Cumberland. The curriculum was six-weeks of classroom courses punctuated with daily exams followed by four months of on-the-job training riding on locomotives with seasoned engineers. Those men filled out written evaluations of their charges after every trip.

Some of them actively mentored their trainees and let them operate the equipment. When the assignment was finished, they'd pat them on the back and warmly say; *If you get another opportunity, come back and ride with me on my turn.*

Others disliked being forced to carry a student with them because the rules stated that an engineer operating without a fireman could get $4 a week in additional salary, and the company would not pay that when a student was riding in the second seat. A few of the engineers resented losing the money and would show their displeasure by generally ignoring the boy. Their good-bye message was: *Well, I'm not going to miss you! You've cost me sixty-four dollars over the past four months.*

After that memorable experience and considerable study, the rookie would return to his studies in the classroom and take a comprehensive written test on locomotive mechanics, safety, operating procedures, train-handling and rules, rules and more rules. Successful completion of the program did not mean that the graduate could move directly into an engineer's job. Instead, his new status only amounted to that of a low-seniority fireman (assistant engineer).

The company would send him out to work on freights for a few months, release him for weeks to return home without pay and later bring him back for a couple of days to fill in for an absent engineer. It was a long, slow trip to a regular engineer's position.

During the first decade of their time with the railroad, firemen, engineers and conductors remained slaves to one of the most stressful labor practices ever conceived. It is used widely and mercilessly by the transportation and health care professions and referred to as "working on call." Under this system, less seniority men and women working off the extra board are kept in a cloud of constant uncertainty, never knowing when the company will contact them to report to work. In railroad service, a "duty call" is a mandatory order, not a request that the employee has the option of declining without severe consequences. Some calls instruct the man to report to a job site up to 100 miles away within two hours.

None of these people can plan for a day off, next week or the one after that. In the days before cell phones, that meant if they left home for a few hours one afternoon to run errands or attended a child's athletic event, they had to take along a roll of quarters and periodically find a pay phone and call in to see if they had been called to work. Such a life translated into a mentally and physically exhausting grind, twenty-four hours a day, seven days a week, with serious repercussions on health and families.

If the fireman stuck it out over those years with good service, he was eventually rewarded with the following call from a company official: *Hey, we are short on engineers and have decided to promote you. You are now a regular engineer.*

That is what he had worked for all those years on-call, a regular assigned run, a turn. Right away, however, the man would sink to the bottom of the engineers' list, last in line for choosing vacation times, first in line for working the days nobody else wanted and vulnerable to furloughs when the railroad business was passing through a slack period. But for the time being he had a relatively secure job with the same hours every day, free from the never know when they gonna want ya routine.

An engineer's or conductor's work hours were another matter. The Hours of Service law, passed by Congress in 1907, mandated that an engineer could not operate a train for more than 16 consecutive hours. It was not until 1974 that the unions convinced Congress to reduce that stretch to 14 hours. By 1977 it was down to 12.

In 1916, railroad labor organizations pressured a pliant President Woodrow Wilson to support the creation of an industry-wide, eight-hour workday. His initial resistance was overcome by the efforts of William Charles Adamson, a U.S. Congressman from rural Carrollton, Georgia, and Chairman of the House Interstate Commerce Committee. Congressman Adamson, a fervent labor supporter, stepped forward and introduced such legislation in the face of an overwhelming outcry from all of the railroad companies.

With the growing probabilities of American intervention in the massive war abroad and a nationwide railroad strike at home, the House and Senate approved the Adamson Railway Labor Act in four days. When Wilson signed the bill into law, it marked the first time in American history that the national government had chosen to regulate the hours of workers employed by private companies.

The law quickly, but barely, survived a constitutional challenge in the U.S. Supreme Court by a 5 to 4 decision and took effect the next year. The language of the ruling, however, did not restrict work days to eight hours but only required employers to pay the men who remained on the job longer, a sum equal to 150% of their normal hourly rate (time and a half) for the extra hours.

The railroad companies knew that they still could require their people to stay on the job for up to 16 hours a day, but they would thereafter have to pay them more for the "overtime." Their objection to the law was based on their premise that the unions were simply jockeying to get their members a pay raise.

In 1938 this historic act was recast into the uniformly accepted concept of a 40-hour work week with overtime pay for any additional time on the job. The unions were eventually credited with the current weekly standard for employees in most lines of work.

The railroad companies, however, found subtle ways to subvert the letter of the new law. In his memoirs, Engineer Deva McCarter, who lived in Florence, S.C., recalled having to work 16 hours a day, 7 days a week on two different trains with only 20 minutes each day for a lunch break. He spent that time sleeping on the floor of the engine cab instead of eating. The company claimed that he was working two different jobs so it didn't have to pay him *any* overtime.

"For sixteen hours you had switchmen going between cars, coupling or un-coupling and working with cumbersome air-brake hoses," he wrote. "If you made one wrong move, someone was going to get hurt. That was a miserable sixteen hours, especially by yourself in the engine with no fireman to help you." [He was talking about the 1960s].

Up until 2008, ten- or twelve-hour shifts, followed by eight hours off, were still the norm for road service (engineers and conductors). The law allowed the company to call men back after eight hours away from the job if they had worked one minute less than twelve. Employees and unions said that was not enough. An average road worker needs half an hour to get home and an hour to get cleaned up and eat dinner. Four-and-one-half hours later, the company could wake him up in the middle of the night with a call to report the next day.

The twelve-hour, split shift still exists as a particularly oppressive practice.. Under these assignments, an engineer can be told to work for six hours with four hours off, followed by another six back on duty. Four hours is too short a period for a man to reach a decent, quiet place and rest, and even though this regimen technically complied with the law, it often meant the engineer was out there operating a train in final hours of his shift with totally inadequate rest.

For over 150 years, railroad managers (not unlike coal mine operators) have wrapped themselves in sacred mantles of unquestionable authority, continually pressing employees to the edges of their physical and mental limits.

In his tersely written and published ethnological study, *The Hoghead* (slang term for an engineer), Dr. Frederick Gamst of the University of Massachusetts wrote, "The carriers have not yet left the militaristic and authoritarian personnel practices of the early Victorian era and continue as a managerial sub-culture analogous to living fossils in the organic realm of nature."

As a result, railroad men and their unions have gained some workplace concessions, but also learned to live with long litanies of heavy-handed punishments for seemingly petty infractions of company rules.

In the mid-1980s, Jack Reed, a fifteen-year veteran engineer in the Maryland Cumberland Division, received a telephone call at home notifying him that he was "four times out" (fourth in line to take a train up or down the road). The caller went on to say that because of scheduling problems, there was only a remote chance he would be summoned that evening. Don't worry about it. With that information, Reed decided to take his wife out to dinner. He was in the restaurant when they rang his house again. It was the first call he had ever missed.

The next day the company ordered him in for a hearing, a little court trial. He arrived wide-eyed and nervous. The verdict was a five-day suspension without pay. He knew it could have been worse; they could have fired him. This heavy-handed enforcement of picayune policies always tends to erase any remaining vestige of employee loyalty to the company. When asked his opinion of his protector union, Reed replied, "I am not a big union supporter, but I believe it is a necessary player in our lives."

He went on to say, "Railroaders live with the fact that some small mistake might be the end of them. If you are a long-term employee in any other occupation and screw up, your boss most likely will take you into his office and chew you out. The railroad, however, is not a discuss-it-with-you, second-chance proposition.

"Say an engineer is backing up an empty, six-car passenger train in the yard at the end of a long day. He can't see anything from up front, but one of his conductors is riding on the rear 'giving him sight' over the radio. The man in the back miscalculates and suddenly the train hits something on the tracks and derails at five miles per hour. No real harm is done, but the next day both conductors and the engineer are going to be looking for another job after 25 years of service. That is the reality that you have to live with. Seniority and unions will not save you."

A modern expression that seems to have originated on the railroad is the term "brownie points." Originally it was a demerit on the personal record of an employee for a violation of the book of rules and was written with dip pen in the conventional brown ink of the time. Today, outside of that culture, its meaning has been morphed into one that implies a kudo, or a job well done.

The older breed of railroaders worked under harsh and risky conditions that left many of their numbers either dead or permanently sidelined with severe injuries at a relatively young age. An overwhelming number did not make it to retirement. Consequently, the men quickly evolved into a thick-skinned bunch of "live today, for tomorrow you may not be here" characters.

Deva McCarter hired-on with the Atlantic Coast Line in 1941. His story was not unusual. It took him twenty years to move from the position of youngest fireman to that of the youngest engineer and then another twenty to make his way to the top twenty on the regular engineers' list. Within his low-country district in South Carolina and Georgia, a surprising number of men never marked off a single day in the course of a year.

In his hand-written memoirs, McCarter recalled that he received $6 a day in the mid-1940s and was delighted when he got a lucrative raise to $15 a day ten years later under a new union contract. Among the amusing stories he recounted was the night that two of his fellow engineers, Cooter Spain and Joe Rhame, were complaining to each other about their bad teeth and the cost of visiting a dentist, drank themselves into oblivion in a stopover town, made a bet and ended up alternately pulling out all of each other's teeth with a pair of pliers. They washed out their mouths with kerosene, slept the night and reported to work the next day.

Another friend of McCarter's, Engineer Fred Pinton, was walking from a crew boarding house in Savannah, Georgia, to a point up the street where the shuttle would pick him up and take him to the rail yard. Along the way a small, stray dog ran up alongside of him snarling and snapping at his pant legs. Pinton kept brushing it away, but the ankle-biter would not leave him alone. Annoyed, he finally reached down and grabbed the animal up in his heavy work gloves. Arriving at his steam engine, he casually climbed up into the cab, opened the roaring firebox and flipped the dog inside.

The jobs of engineer and to a lesser extent, conductor and brakeman, share one thing in common with police officers and firemen. They all have extended periods of routine tedium punctuated with unexpected moments of sudden terror.

Opha Herdman, a former brakeman with the New York Central working the rails in his home state of West Virginia, remembered riding in the engine cab of a freight one night in 1955. The crew was pulling 30 gondolas of coal around and across the Blue Creek Gorge from High Top to Charleston. Since the train's air brakes were not working very well that day, Opha had partially tied-down the hand brakes on four of the cars.

"Our engineer, John Hammick, was an older man with diminished eyesight and hearing," he remembered. "We were rolling downhill into a right-to-left curve where he couldn't see ahead. The fireman was dead asleep on the left side of the locomotive cab and I was sitting behind him. I happened to glance up the line, saw something in the moonlight moving on the upcoming bridge over the river and broke out yelling, 'Emergency! Emergency!'

"John, was slow to react but he finally 'knocked em in the head' (hit the emergency brake). It seemed like we slid forever before coming to a stop on the trestle, six feet from a large horse that had apparently walked out on the bridge and dropped down through the ties up to its chest with all four legs dangling below. If we had hit the thing, the train would have de-railed and we all would have ended up at the bottom of that gorge.

"The conductor came up from the caboose. We got our lanterns and walked for over a mile up the line banging on every farmhouse door until we finally found the man that was missing a horse. He handed me a shotgun and said, 'You boys have my permission to shoot the animal.'

"'No sir,' I said. "The company would find out, pay you money for it, and fire us. You got to go up there and shoot him yourself.'

"It was a mess. We found a logging chain, wrapped it around the remains of the horse, secured it to the engine and pulled him out of the ties and tracks. The whole job must have taken an hour."

From region to region, and decade to decade, the stories are similar and abundant. Train crews have always relied on grim toughness and quick reflexes to deal with the peculiar demands of their jobs.

As Jack Reed, the Cumberland Division engineer put it, "When you're dropping down the seven-mile grade from Bardane to Harpers Ferry, West Virginia in a freight loaded with 18,000 tons of coal and less than 100 feet, or less, of visibility in the fog, you better have your balls in your back pocket. Even at a slow speed, you may get 'er stopped if you have to, but the range of other possibilities will make your butt pucker."

For the highest seniority men, salary and benefits have never been bad. An eight-hour day in 1996 paid $154 for a job covering up to 100 miles. But few settled for that. Engineers and conductors in passenger service who were able to do double-runs each day got paid twice that much, maybe $1400 a week. That was $72,800 a year with five weeks' paid vacation and eleven paid "personal leave" days. A few of the freight men stretched it to the limit working 12 hours a day, seven days a week, and made $100,000 in one year. In reality, the average is still probably in the $75,000 range for those who want to have some semblance of a home life.

Ricky Orr's chosen path from brakeman to engineer trainee was a fortuitous one. Just one year after signing on, he was "promoted engineer" (in 1974) and began operating freight trains. Since road-service positions were highly competitive, he had to settle for switching jobs back in the Baltimore yards. There he found himself again working with Bly, Quillen and Major.

Eight years later he was back on the road moving freights between Baltimore, Washington and Brunswick, Maryland. In

1994, he made the transition to regular passenger service. On the first of January, 1996 (six weeks before the accident that would alter so many lives), Orr successfully bid and received the regular engineer turn on a MARC commuter train that ran the Baltimore to Washington to Brunswick roundtrip circuit.

Trim and muscular, he looked years younger than forty-three. Lightning-fast physical and mental reflexes successfully propelled him through a variety of weekend sports such as power-boating, bicycling, motorcycling, and sailing. According to those who knew him, he was always a pleasure to work with, one of those guys who was serious about his job but could also keep you laughing. With two broken marriages in his wake, he was again the bachelor engineer wearing multiple gold rings and necklaces.

Women, old and young, were attracted to him, not because of the jewelry, but his considerate demeanor and affable personality. Orr kept up his membership in every social organization in his area. He was a Lion, a Moose and a Mason and fraternized with the sororities that were affiliated with those groups. According to those that knew him best, however, his only true love was the railroad.

Russell Bly couldn't say enough about Orr's talents. "I would compare his skills to those of an ace test-pilot or a super NASCAR driver. He could make locomotives do things that other guys couldn't even think about. On a cold rainy night facing a steep grade with fifty cars and one motor (locomotive), most engineers would say, 'Forget it, we're going to have to take them up in three or four cuts. Even with the wheel sanders spittin' grit on the tracks, we couldn't get no traction.'

"Ricky, however, knew how to use the right amount of brake-pressure to avoid the wheel-slips, knew how to keep the amperage up and how to get-a-hold of fifty cars with the one motor and go.

"He had the feelin' in his ass when he sat down in the engineer's seat, like physically becoming part of the entire train behind him. We admired and trusted his ability. When he was 'running light' with just an engine and a few cars and had to get it stopped without burning up the engine-brake pads, he knew all the tricks. He would reverse the thing to get the wheels pulling the other way to get her stopped."

Years later, one of Orr's supervisors, a CSXT passenger operations manager, spoke highly of him. "He was one of the most professional engineers that we had out there. He did a real good job in everything. He was always consistent and always concise."

His skills would soon meet their ultimate test.

Five

Union Station, Washington D.C.
February 16, 1996, 1:24 p.m.

For the second leg of their trip, the one to Brunswick, Ricky
Orr, Jimmy Major and Jim Quillen got their train moving out
of Union Station and the Washington Terminal Yard twenty-
four minutes behind schedule. They had only four scheduled
stops along the route, but ominous weather predictions had
encouraged a crush of commuters who usually rode later
trains to leave work early and pile onto theirs. The MARC
crew, according to railroad practice, was obliged to honor
individual passenger requests to let them off at any of the
unscheduled stations along the way. An hour and a half later,
the train finally arrived in Brunswick.

At this point in their lives, twenty-five years after they
started working together, each of the three original Crew
members had developed their own special eccentricities and
interests. Jim Quillen, 53, carried and read a bible every day on
the job. He was on fire for Jesus Christ and was working to
win over souls on the railroad. Ricky Orr, 43, was one of his
tentative converts and attended Jim's church in Frederick.

Quillen's twelve-year-old son had a congenital heart defect, and the compassionate father was heavily involved in activities with him. They worked together on weekends building model planes. Jim was also an assistant scout master of the boy's troop #792 on Ballenger Creek Pike outside of Frederick.

Jimmy Major was 48. He and his 17-year-old son were into restoring antique cars. They had completed work on a red, 1965 Mustang and were rebuilding an old Chevrolet pickup truck that Ricky Orr had given them. That project had taken three years, and the father and son were almost finished. A neighbor said, "It was like a jewel in their garage."

Orr, had discovered a unique and all-consuming hobby, raising and selling racing (homing) pigeons. It was serious. He even marketed and shipped some of them overseas. Russell Bly figured that *the boy had a pile of birds*, because Orr not only built three coops in his back yard but would borrow Bly's pickup truck every other weekend to haul a ton of feed.

Ricky, however, was living by himself. Four months previously his second wife had moved back to New York with her son, a sixth grader. He had, however, faithfully helped to support his nineteen-year-old son, Christopher, by his first marriage. The young man lived in Baltimore and worked for the Giant Foods grocery chain.

Walking into the small wooden station in Brunswick, Orr, Major and Quillen bumped into two of their fellow railroaders, Engineer Jobe Breeden and Conductor Leechel Reynolds. Those men were about to take a MARC train back into Washington. The five men spent a few minutes discussing the new, consolidated seniority roster. The consensus was that the plan was being shoved down their throats by both CSXT and the unions without sufficient input from employees.

The Crew then climbed into a company van and rode up the steep hills behind Brunswick to the Green Country Inn for a late lunch. Several years after its old, downtown boarding house for railroad workers had burned down, the local YMCA had financed and built an attractive new motel and restaurant near the Brunswick High School. The railroad still needed a nice place to house and feed its crewmembers while they were in town, so it contracted with the motel to reserve 20 of its rooms for them.

An outfit called Motel Sleepers eventually took over management of the place and opened the other 40 rooms, restaurant and fitness center to the general public. When railroaders were sidelined for a few hours or overnight, they could repair there to eat a good meal, take a nap in the lobby or check into a room. Itinerant construction employees stuck around the area for extended work assignments usually made up the balance of the tenants. In 1996, a man could get a room for $42 a night, $187 a week or $630 a month and enjoy "home style" cooking, 24 hours a day, at the Green Country Diner next to the motel lobby.

After lunch, the three returned to the Brunswick station. Jim Quillen, as he did every day, called his wife Betty. Ricky Orr broke away from the others and walked a block up the street to the antique shop owned by Brunswick city councilman Jim Castle. He and Jim often spent time talking about their mutual interest in railroad memorabilia (especially watches) while Ricky was waiting to start his trip back to Washington. That day he didn't linger and told Jim that he was "short on time" and would talk to him next week.

Six

In the course of their careers, Jim Quillen, Jimmy Major and Ricky Orr operated trains over the two hundred miles of lines that had once comprised the original core of the first American transportation empire. In 1827, a small group of Baltimore businessmen secured charters from the states of Maryland and Virginia, raised $3 million in public and private funds and began planning an east-west rail line which would eventually link the port city of Baltimore to the Ohio River.

They began construction of their Baltimore and Ohio (B&O) Railroad on July 4, 1828, exactly two years to the day after former presidents Thomas Jefferson and John Adams had both died. The last surviving signer of the Declaration of Independence, ninety-year-old Charles Carroll of Maryland, accepted the honor of turning the first spade of earth at a spot where the line was to begin - on ten acres dedicated to the project by a Carroll cousin on his the *Mount Clare* farm in today's downtown Baltimore.

It took work crews two years to sculpt the B&O's initial roadbed westward a mere twelve miles along the Patapsco River gorge to the small industrial village of Ellicott's Mills (now Ellicott City). The following year they extended the tracks an additional forty-nine across rolling farmlands to the fields outside of Frederick, Maryland.

During its first four years of operations, the company used horses to pull passenger carriages, similar to stage coaches, and a simple freight car over thin iron straps attached to stone foundations. In 1833 the B&O replaced the animals with primitive steam engines and began building a forty-mile branch line to Washington using metal "T" rails imported from England.

Twenty-four months later the B&O was moving about 200 people a day between its Baltimore's Mt. Clare depot (the current site of the B&O Railroad Museum) and a converted wooden boarding house serving as a terminal on the first block of Pennsylvania Avenue within a stone's throw of the U.S. Capitol building.

A one-way trip took two hours and cost $2.50 ($78 in today's currency). At that rate, businessmen proved to be their primary clientele. Each train made local stops along the route and observed a City of Baltimore ordinance that mandated the use of horses to move the cars on tracks within the downtown to avoid disrupting the large population of other animals drawing wagons and carriages. In its first full year of operation, the new Washington Branch earned revenues of $176,000 ($5.46 million today) from 75,400 passengers. That worked out to be an amazing 50% profit.

The company soon realized that its financial future was not just in passenger service, but also in the delivery of natural resources from west of the Allegheny Mountains to the east coast. To secure the necessary capital to continue expanding in that direction, the B&O issued stocks and bonds. The State of Maryland, the City of Baltimore and private investors each purchased one-third of them, and the three groups were entitled to select a proportionate number (12) of the 36 B&O board members. No federal funds or land grants were solicited or offered. The national government did, however, assist the young railway enterprise by allowing the U.S. Army Corps of Engineers to work in planning and surveying its route. By 1842 trains were running through to Cumberland, Maryland, 178 miles west of Baltimore.

Freight quickly proved to be the railroad's largest profit generator. Forty-two percent of the cargo coming into Baltimore was coal, followed by flour, livestock, iron, stone and tobacco. In 1845, the company again used bonds to finance the construction of a new deep-water terminal on a half-mile stretch of waterfront property near the downtown at Locust Point. There they could transfer coal, grain and merchandise to ships serving most of the Eastern states.

In 1852 the B&O completed the last 200 miles of its main "stem" line from Cumberland to the Ohio River at Wheeling, Virginia. Investors were ecstatic; their new company was experiencing phenomenal financial success, and its board of directors began declaring annual stock dividends ranging from 6 to 8 percent.

One of the early patrons of the young railroad was a wealthy Baltimore businessman. Years earlier, in 1807, his devout Quaker parents had turned a highly successful tobacco plantation in nearby Anne Arundel County, Maryland (Annapolis is the county seat) into a marginal operation overnight when they freed the family's slaves. With the labor gone, their twelve-year-old son was taken out of school and required to work in the fields with his parents. Five years later the boy's father decided to allow him to move into downtown Baltimore and work for his Uncle Gerald, a wholesale grocer and commission merchant.

Over time, the young man proved to be a very savvy businessman, even to the point of disagreeing with his uncle over his policy of refusing to accommodate rural customers who wished to pay for their purchases with generous amounts of homemade liquor. When the two eventually parted company, a gracious Gerald loaned his nephew enough money to start his own, independent commission operation. The fledgling entrepreneur began accepting moonshine in trade and reselling it under his own label, despite the fact that the local Society of Friends (Quakers) temporarily turned him out of their meeting.

His wholesale grocery company began prospering after three of his brothers joined him as salesmen. The four of them expanded their customer base throughout Maryland, Virginia (focusing on the agriculturally rich Shenandoah Valley) and Eastern North Carolina.

After twenty-five years as one of the most successful businessmen on the East Coast, he was done. He retired, and began spending time investing his profits in banking and venture-capital lending. He especially favored energetic young men who possessed innovative business ideas but could not secure start-up loans from local banks.

The Baltimore and Ohio Railroad was one of his favorite bets, and he started buying large quantities of Baltimore and Ohio Railroad stock. In 1847, the company's board of directors asked him, at age 52, to fill one of their vacant seats. Eight years after that the same body elected him chairman of their powerful finance committee - a position he held for the next twenty-six years. During that period he risked his personal fortune to help the B&O weather severe financial difficulties by personally endorsing its notes. On several occasions, he even served as president pro tempore of the company and signed stock certificates. His strong Quaker abolitionist sentiments (not to mention his substantial investment) led him to work tirelessly during the Civil War to keep the B&O lines securely in the hands of the federal government.

When the new Union State of West Virginia was formed at the mid-point of the war (1863), the counties of Jefferson and Berkeley, strongly linked to the other Tidewater areas of Virginia with plantation-style agricultural economies, use of slaves and the dominant Episcopal faith, was summarily removed from Virginia and included in the West state only because the B&O Railroad's main line ran through them from Harpers Ferry to Martinsburg.

By the time of his death in 1873 at age 77, Mr. Johns Hopkins (Johns was a family surname) had never married, had never spoken before an audience in public, and except for holding lavish dinner parties for his extended family and circle of friends, had always lived an ascetic life.

At the same time, however, he had acquired the greatest number of shares of Baltimore and Ohio Railroad stock ever owned by a private individual. His will specified that $5 million of his $8 million estate ($4.5 billion today) be used by selected Quaker trustees to build and endow a university and "free teaching hospital" in downtown Baltimore - a project that he had personally established on paper a few years earlier. Up until that point, endowments to individual universities in the United States, including Harvard, Princeton and Cornell, had not exceeded $500,000.

Although the Civil War brought railroad construction to a four-year standstill, the business climate that followed it proved to be ideal for national economic development. In 1865, John Work Garrett, B&O president and best friend of Johns Hopkins, began searching for possible expansion opportunities. He soon discovered and purchased the defunct charter of a Maryland line that had not progressed beyond its planning stage.

The history of this short line dated back to 1853 when a coalition of businessmen in Washington and adjacent Montgomery County, Maryland, incorporated a company called *The Metropolitan Railroad.* Its mission was to build a rail link northwest from the nation's capital to a spot on the Baltimore and Ohio's main line in Western Maryland east of of Brunswick. On paper it looked like a logical shortcut for Washington-area residents to travel east and west without enduring the longer route through Baltimore. The group was not able, however, to raise enough capital to begin the project.

What revived the project under Garrett's leadership was a strong competitive move by the B&O's archrival, the Pennsylvania Railroad. Between 1866 and 1872, the Penn or "Pennsy," not only established a passenger route from Philadelphia to Baltimore and Washington D.C., but also managed to secure exclusive rights to run their trains across the Potomac River using the "Long Bridge," the only direct access from Washington to the Southern states. That span, built in 1809, was located where the 14th Street Metro subway and railroad bridges are today.

This bold maneuver in the B&O's backyard prompted Garrett to buy and activate the old Metropolitan charter and start building the Washington and Metropolitan Branch, or "Met." By 1873 this new connecting line joined Washington D.C. to the original stem line at Point of Rocks, 43 miles to the northwest. All B&O passenger-trains traveling to and from the large mid-western cities began using it for service into the District of Columbia and up the Washington Branch to Baltimore.

Tracts of land along the first sixteen miles of the new Met Line between Washington and Rockville, Maryland, soon became a hot target for developers. By 1887, speculators had laid out the new community of Garrett Park (named for the venerable B&O chief executive who recently had died) and started marketing it as a Washington version of New York's exclusive Tuxedo Park and Philadelphia's suburban Bryn Mawr.

At the same time, businessmen changed the name of Knowles Station, located between Rockville and Silver Spring, to "Kensington," a more fashionable British title, and began building period frame houses throughout the woods south of the tracks there. Nearby Forest Glen was soon promoted as a summer resort while a group of Washington-area Methodists developed Washington Grove near Gaithersburg as a summer camp-meeting site.

John Garrett's son, Robert, succeeded him as president in 1884 and enthusiastically continued the company's policy of aggressive growth. Over the next two years he oversaw both the completion of an expensive ($20 million) 111-mile line from Baltimore to Philadelphia and the opening of the Curtis Bay coal port and terminal adjacent to Baltimore. Those far-reaching and expensive projects, coupled with the financial depression of 1893, pushed the company slowly over the edge into insolvency. In 1896, receivers mandated a harsh corporate reorganization, but even that did not dampen the B&O managers from planning an offensive that would soon more than double the size of their network. In effect, they just legally stiffed most of their creditors.

The next three presidents expanded the system from 2,095 to 4,434 miles of track with acquisitions and route extensions in western Pennsylvania, Ohio, Indiana, Illinois and New York. They could not ignore the looming race with other lines to get bigger, faster.

Since the Pennsylvania Railroad had effectively blocked any competitors from gaining access across the Potomac River at Washington, the B&O decided to construct its own bridge across the river in the 1890s. The plan was to branch off the Met at a point one mile west of Silver Spring, swing south around the northwestern boundary of Washington through Chevy Chase and Bethesda, cross the Potomac near Chain Bridge, rise up into the Virginia palisades through the Pimmit

Run ravine (a point on the George Washington Parkway today) and run southwest to Fairfax Station. There it could connect with the Richmond and Danville (later the Southern Railway).

Even though their anticipated bridge over the Potomac was never built, the company did go ahead and complete an 11-mile branch to the edge of the river and down its bank into a western enclave of Washington called Georgetown. This "Metropolitan Southern Railroad" was completed in 1910. The northern connection point of the line joined with the Met near Silver Spring, and was named *Georgetown Junction*.

The short Georgetown branch operated profitably until the 1960s when the B&O Company abandoned portions of it. By 1986 the entire line was out of service and Georgetown Junction was a junction in name only. Most of its old rail bed is now a bicycle and walking path called the Capital Crescent Trail.

By the year 1916, the national Baltimore and Ohio system controlled 4,500 miles of roadway, employed 60,000 people and earned $11.7 million. That equated to 13.4 employees and $26,000 in revenue for each mile of track (over $250,000 per mile in 2009 dollars). The national average for railroads at the time was only 6.6 workers and $14,500 per mile.

In the mid-1920s, Daniel Willard, the longest-serving B&O president (1910-1941), inaugurated two all-Pullman trains that ran every day over the Met. *The Capitol Limited* linked New York, Washington Pittsburgh and Chicago, and the *National Limited* ran to and from Washington, and the Midwest, primarily the cities of Cincinnati and St. Louis. These "through" runs offered luxury features such as state-of-the-art sleeping accommodations, swanky lounges, secretarial services, on-call nurse, valets, maids, barber, manicurist and shower baths.

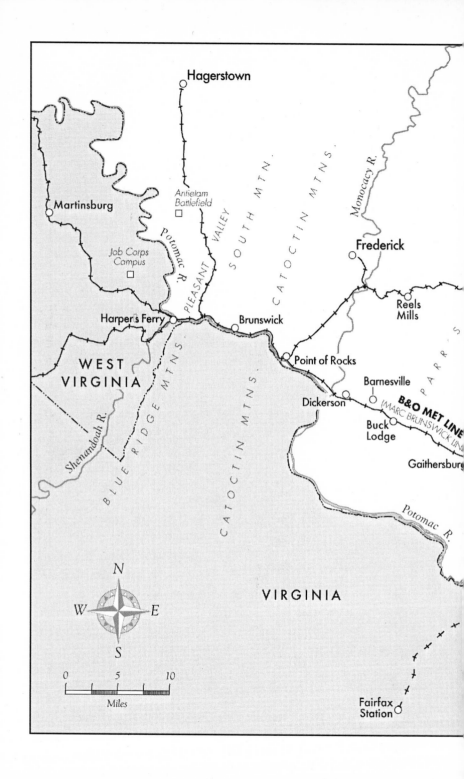

The Baltimore and Ohio Railroad in Maryland

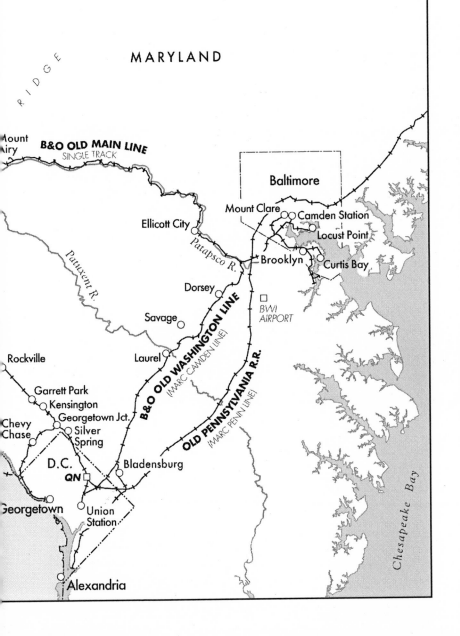

MARYLAND

B&O OLD MAIN LINE
SINGLE TRACK

Mount Airy

RIDGE

Baltimore

Mount Clare
Camden Station
Locust Point

Ellicott City

Patapsco R.

Brooklyn
Curtis Bay

Patuxent R.

Dorsey

Savage

BWI AIRPORT

Rockville

Laurel

B&O OLD WASHINGTON LINE
(MARC CAMDEN LINE)

OLD PENNSYLVANIA R.R.
(MARC PENN LINE)

Garrett Park
Kensington
Chevy Chase
Georgetown Jct.
Silver Spring

D.C.
QN

Bladensburg

Georgetown

Union Station

Alexandria

Chesapeake Bay

After years of attempting to operate their own sleeping cars, the B&O eventually followed the example of other lines and leased them from the Pullman Company. Its coaches were highly popular with travelers because they offered clean, private accommodations serviced by an army of impeccably trained porters. Since Pullman had a policy of hiring black men to work those well-respected jobs, the company soon became the largest employer of African Americans in the United States.

In 1927 Willard orchestrated 365-days of birthday parties and oversaw the manufacture of a magnificent line of blue commemorative dining china. The Baltimore and Ohio was 100 years old. Over the next few years, prosperity reigned as the carrier moved an average of 17,500 passengers a month and enjoyed an "on- time" record of 95.4 percent.

The onset of the Great Depression, however, forced the Baltimore and Ohio to severely reduce its workforce, and by 1933 its employment roster was less than half of what it had been in 1927. By 1936, local commuter operations had all but vanished on the Met, and only long-distance passenger trains and freights were using the line between Washington and points west. The company arranged to borrow $4.5 million for nine years at 4% interest (a $3 billion "bailout" in today's parlance) from Roosevelt's Public Works Administration.

The 1930s, however, were not totally bleak for passenger operations. During the middle years of that decade, the B&O kept initiating improvements such as the first completely air-conditioned passenger train, *The Columbian*, that ran between Washington and New York. Within the next twelve months they expanded that amenity to sleepers on *The National Limited* and *Capitol Limited* and soon decided to equip its entire fleet of 275 passenger cars with AC. In 1937 they inaugurated the country's first "streamlined" road-passenger locomotives. This new design trend was simple to implement by retrofitting the locomotives with metal shrouds to give them a sleek, aerodynamic appearance.

The interiors of the passenger cars were appointed in the fashionable Art Deco styling and accessories. *The Capitol's* "Martha Washington" dining cars featured a Chesapeake Bay cuisine, and cars exhibited leaded-glass windows, chandeliers, and colonial furnishings. Sleeping accommodations cost about $4 a night and a full dinner served by a steward started at 60 cents. As late as 1938, a roundtrip fare between Washington and New York City was $3.75. Five bucks would get you the roundtrip ride with breakfast going and dinner coming back. Most fares were advertised in the range of 2 cents a mile.

America's entrance into the Second World War jerked the B&O out of its financial slump but at the same time presented it with other serious problems. While the demand for rail travel increased dramatically, thousands of men left their jobs to join the armed services, and the company was soon looking at 34,000 vacant positions. It quickly began recruiting women to fill many of them. The ladies worked in stations, offices and out on the lines in track maintenance operations. The absence of unskilled labor, on the other hand, became so acute that management arranged, through the federal government, for the temporary importation and employment of 2,800 Mexican nationals.

The national crisis required that military and civilian goods be routed around the country as quickly as possible, and the Brunswick-to-Washington Met line suddenly became a high-volume, fast-freight route. The number of passengers riding over the B&O's lines nationwide reached totals never before imagined. During the forty-five months of war (1941-1945) 113,891 special troop trains moved an average of one million men per month.

After the war and into the early 1950s, spiraling operating costs and declining passenger revenues forced the B&O to cancel 100 scheduled passenger trains and cut employment rolls by a whopping 81%. The men that kept their jobs were those with the highest-seniority, and their wages continued to increase 5% a year for the remainder of the decade.

What eventually brought down the final curtain on the golden age of passenger trains was the debut of the affordable automobile. In just four, post-war years, 1945 to 1949, returning veterans bought more than five million. By 1952, forty million households were driving home an astounding eight million a year. Gasoline was cheap, about 20 cents a gallon, and the supply appeared to be endless.

By 1955, the Baltimore and Ohio Company's balance sheet began bleeding red ink, an accumulated passenger-service deficit of $13 million. Even with that burden, it fought hard to hang on and continue to court rail patrons when other railroads were abandoning them. What set its passenger trains apart from their competitors during those postwar years was its service. Management did not compromise their ethic of providing courteous and attentive staff and well-maintained coaches. Only fresh vegetables, no canned or frozen food at all, were served in the dining cars. The B&O also continued its tradition of treating its employees with dignity. Such corporate behavior was often missing on other lines.

An example of this was the story of Edward Lee Moore, a B&O employee who worked as a crossing watchman in the Brunswick area. Before the installation of automatic gates and flashing red lights, crossing watchmen stood at points where busy roads intersected rail lines. They took shelter in small shacks and remained prepared to stop automobile traffic when a train was approaching.

Moore's granddaughter, Brunswick native and railroader Winnie Hane, worked her way up from the job of car-man's helper cleaning out emptied freight cars in the yards, to Amtrak conductor. She could not remember the details of the crossing accident in which her grandfather lost the use of both of his legs, but she did recall the Baltimore and Ohio Company's response. It offered Moore a choice of several new-career training opportunities. He selected watch repairing, and the company sent him to Buchanan, West Virginia, to learn that trade.

Moore's return to Brunswick happened to coincide with the retirement of the local jewelry store's proprietor. The railroad company immediately bought the business on West Potomac Street and turned it over to Moore. He lived out the rest of his days repairing clocks and railroaders' watches. In fact, the B&O designated him as the official company "watch inspector" in Brunswick, a lucrative title since every railroad man was required to have his watch periodically inspected.

B&O President Willard had set the company's official attitude and tone decades earlier with widely-circulated public statements like; "It will be the policy of the Baltimore and Ohio Railroad Company to endeavor to do efficiently all the things that a public servant should do....It is our desire that people living along our lines should feel that the B&O is a good neighbor. If they are ever visited by fire, flood or epidemic, they should instinctively call upon us first for assistance, because of our potential strength and willingness to help them."

Though its relationship with its employees and the public remained outstanding, the B&O's financial woes continued to mount. Both of its primary east-west rivals, the Chesapeake and Ohio and New York Central Lines, began competing to either merge with the B&O or take it over.

By 1961, the C&O had both the cash and the sympathy of existing B&O shareholders and employees to purchase 70% of the ailing company's stock, and on New Years' Eve, 1962, the U.S. Interstate Commerce Commission approved Chesapeake and Ohio Railroad's petition to take over the B&O and rescue it from imminent bankruptcy. To continue to capitalize on the "brand" of the company that it had just acquired, the C&O decided to maintain the B&O corporate name and logo on those engines, cars and appurtenances.

By the early 1970s, commuter traffic on the Brunswick and Washington line began to increase. The recently completed I-270 running on a north-south route between Washington and Frederick, Maryland, had stimulated the construction of tens of thousands of new homes along its corridor and brought twice that number of automobiles. Suburbanites did not stop at Frederick but moved even further westward past Brunswick into the panhandle of West Virginia.

The new four-lane interstate quickly proved inadequate to efficiently handle morning and evening traffic, and many commuters started looking to the railroad as a practical, comfortable and inexpensive alternative. Soon they were able to use it to connect with Washington's new Metro subway system (begun in 1976) at Union Station and access most of the employment centers throughout the capital city and adjoining Arlington County and City of Alexandria across the Potomac River.

This, in conjunction with a major financial subsidy from the State of Maryland and a lesser one with the State of West Virginia, increased commuter service on the Brunswick (Met) Line to nine Washington trains a day, seven each way from Brunswick and two more from Martinsburg, West Virginia.

The 1970s were also the years of accelerated rail mergers and consolidations. The venerable lines of the past quickly became relics of bygone glory, consigned to the board game *Monopoly* and the nostalgic creations of model railroaders.

Soon after the C&O purchased both the B&O and the 800-mile-long Western Maryland Railroad that came with it, the C&O too was acquired in the winter of 1973 by a "holding company" called the Chessie System. A holding company is a team of investors that pools its money to buy enough public voting stock in a corporation to control its management and business plan. They achieve that by replacing a majority of the board of directors with people that will do their bidding. Holding companies are also called parent companies.

Seven years later, the mix changed again. Another holding company, the CSX Corporation of Richmond, Virginia, took over both the Seaboard Coast Line (former *Seaboard Airline* and *Atlantic Coast Line* headquartered in Jacksonville, Florida) and the Chessie System based in Cleveland, Ohio.

The CSX acronym was most likely formed from the names of the (C)hessie, and the (S)eaboard. Since these two entities also brought other holdings with them such as the historic Greenbrier Hotel in West Virginia, the new CS conglomerate added an (X) to represent either "all other" or "eXtended family. In July of 1986 the company created a separate unit for its rolling stock called CSX Transportation or CSXT. Within a year, all of the older railroad "families" finally lost their historic identities. At that time, the nation's senior common carrier, the 160 year-old Baltimore and Ohio, ceased to exist as a named railroad.

CSX established its operational headquarters in the former Atlantic Coast Line high-rise office building in downtown Jacksonville, and immediately became the nation's fifth largest railroad. Within a few years 35,000 employees were daily managing rail transportation and distribution services over a consolidated 21,000-mile network encompassing 42,700 actual miles of track (all branches added) in 23 states east of the Mississippi River. In the final years of the first decade of the twenty-first century CSXT was moving 1,700 trains a day with an inventory of 3,800 locomotives and 104,000 freight cars.

CSXT also inherited a good portion of the rights-of-way (Brunswick and Camden Lines) over which the State of Maryland operated its 187-mile commuter-rail service. That meant that it could dictate the terms of its use. The Penn Line tracks used by the commuter system are controlled by Amtrak.

In 1976, the State of Maryland established a public railroad administration to oversee all state and federal commuter-rail subsidies, purchase new equipment and assist commercial short-lines. Five years later the legislature voted to continue financing regional commuter operations as long as passenger fares paid for 50 percent of the costs. A 1984 study resulted in branding the state-supported commuter-rail services with the acronym MARC (for Maryland Area Rail Commuter). The State Railroad Administration became part of the Maryland Mass Transit Administration (MTA) in 1992.

Today, MARC is the commuter-rail arm of the MTA.

All of the engineers and conductors that operate commuter trains on the three MARC lines are CSX employees. Under a contractual arrangement, the MTA pays the costs of their positions and gives CSX 6.5 percent of commuter ticket revenues. CSX provides dispatching services, equipment maintenance and train-crew supervision. The conductors wear dark blue MARC uniforms, logo jackets and traditional hats while the engineers dress anyway they prefer, usually blue jeans and sport shirts.

Under the terms of their operating agreement with MARC, CSX is insulated against any monetary damages that might arise from injuries suffered by commuters or its employees. The state covers the passenger risk through the purchase of commercial insurance for the first $150 million of passenger-related liabilities and pays CSXT a substantial surcharge on top of their billings to insure *its* workers. In 1996 (the year of the accident) 40 MARC commuter trains owned by the MTA transported approximately 19,000 people every weekday. Ten years later that number had risen to over 30,000.

Everything had been running well for years. No one could have imagined what was coming.

Seven

February 16, 1996
4:15 p.m.

The National Weather Service updated its forecast:

Travel should be avoided since roads are already jammed with
people trying to get home. Moderate to heavy snow will continue
into the evening hours and taper to light snow or flurries. Total
accumulation will rise from 8 to 14 inches. Temperatures will fall
to the middle 20s by 11 p.m. Winds will be northeast 20 to 30
miles per hour, which will cause some blowing and drifting and
reduced visibility.

For the trip back to Union Station from Brunswick, the
MARC train operated by Ricky Orr, Jim Quillen and Jimmy
Major was designated the P286. Scheduled to leave at 4:30, the
P286 was basically returning empty passenger-cars back to
Washington to pick up commuters at Union Station and
shuttle them out the Baltimore-Camden Line at the end of the
work day. It seldom boarded any more than a handful of
riders at Brunswick or the other interim flag stops into D.C. at
that time of day.

Friday, the 16th of February, however, was the eve of the
Presidents Day holiday weekend, and eighteen students
attending the federal Jobs Corps school near Harpers Ferry

were driven thirteen miles to the Brunswick railroad station in two school vans. Those select few had earned passes to go home for the next three days. All of them lived in the metropolitan areas of Washington, Baltimore or Philadelphia.

The Harpers Ferry Center is located on a rural campus 70 miles northwest of Washington, D.C., a few miles across the fields and rolling hills from the southern bank of the upper Potomac River. Its classroom, administrative, dormitory and athletic buildings are spread over 77 pastoral acres in Jefferson County, West Virginia, and was one of many created by the Economic Opportunity Act of 1966 – part of President Lyndon Johnson's "War on Poverty." Nationwide, the U.S. Department of Labor staffs, equips and operates 110 such centers designed to prepare approximately 40,000 students a year for quality, blue-collar jobs. Many graduates go on to achieve college degrees.

The facility can house up to 210 attendees, but in early 1996 it had approximately 120. Its student profile has always been young men and women, ages 16 to 24, who have voluntarily enrolled in a one- to two-year regimen of studies and intensive job-skills training. The school's core requirement dictates that all of its students initially work to obtain a GED certification – the nationally recognized test that can prove one possesses academic skills equivalent to those held by most high school graduates. That will enable them to pursue additional training and secure employment certifications in fields such as brick masonry, carpentry, painting, business, computer skills, healthcare, clerical and building maintenance.

The program recruits personally motivated, but "at risk," young people who have dropped out of high school and never held a full-time job. The educational format is supplemented with instruction in self-discipline and workplace deportment, and reinforced with strong personal encouragement. The center also provides its students with lodging, three meals a day, a clothing allowance and a modest weekly cash stipend. They can also earn minimum-wage salaries working on training assignments out in the community at large. In 1996, qualification for trips home on minor holidays was based on a strict system of personal performance (merits and demerits) similar to a military school.

Corps supporters say seven of ten students successfully complete their coursework and secure full-time employment or continue their education. The job-placement rate, according to U.S. Senator Barbara Mikulski of Maryland, is higher than that at Harvard. Skeptics have argued that only one-half of those enrolled meet that standard. Either way the program has proved to be a sound investment in American youth.

On Friday, the 16th of February, the sixteen young men and two young women arrived at the Brunswick train station at 4:15 p.m. Some of them were traveling outside of Harpers Ferry for the first time since they started with the Corps. Lining up at the window inside the Victorian, burgundy-colored station, they presented their vouchers to the stationmaster, received their tickets and walked out the door through the falling snow to the waiting train.

The front MARC passenger car was the only one that was open, so they all filed into it. The five or six who had taken the trip before stretched out on the long orange-and-blue, three-passenger seats and relaxed. The others, most of whom had never been inside a train, stood in the aisle and excitedly talked about what they were going to do when they got home. All but three were nineteen years old or younger.

MARC railroad crews often transported Maryland and West Virginia school classes into Washington D.C., usually during the spring months, and they treated them all the same. The students were given an entire coach to themselves. The only bathroom on the train that day was also located in the first car.

The group included nineteen-year-old Damian Benitez, his buddies called him Danny; Rodney Crawford, also 19; Tyrai Boyer, 16, and Eric Garcia, 18. Benitez sat down and started listening to his walkman with earplugs. Crawford paced up and down the aisle chatting. He and Michael Woodson, nicknamed "the bull" because of his bulky athletic frame, had plans to take a Greyhound bus from Washington to Philadelphia. Crawford asked Woodson if he would help him once they got to Washington.

Woodson assured him, "Yeah, I'm going to show you the way home. The bus station is a short walk from the train station, and I don't live that far from where you're going."

At seventeen, Woodson was a dormitory leader and an avid basketball player. He had received numerous academic awards and the honor of being "student-of-the-month" on several occasions. His goal was to be a master brick mason. The previous summer he had volunteered to help build a new animal shelter for the City of Martinsburg, West Virginia, just up the road from the school. The center's staff characterized him as the boy who was always smiling and willing to help others.

The two young girls, Lakeisha Marshall of Capital Heights, Maryland, and Diana Hanvichid of Woodbridge, Virginia, walked to the middle section of the car away from the others. They were both seventeen. Lakeisha was called "Kie-Kee" by her friends, had been studying at the school for nine months and recently certified by the State of West Virginia as a nursing assistant. Her ambition was to be a licensed practical nurse. Like Michael Woodson, Kie-Kee was a dorm leader, serious about her studies. Her peers often commented about her outgoing personality and infectious sense of humor.

Diana started at the Harpers Ferry campus eleven months earlier. She too was enrolled in the Health Occupations program and worked part-time at a local nursing home in nearby Charles Town. Her parents were Laotian emigrants, and her sister was a practicing physician in that country. Diana was born in nearby Thailand. She was planning to run for a position in the Job Corps student government later in the year and had expressed a desire to attend medical school after graduation.

Eighteen-year-old Carlos Byrd walked up the aisle and sat down near the two girls. He was from Baltimore and had been immersed in the healthcare curriculum for six and a half months. He shared Diana's dream of becoming a physician. As one of the dormitory leaders, he particularly enjoyed mentoring and motivating those around him who were struggling. Byrd had joined Woodson as a starter on the Center's basketball team.

Seventeen-year-old Ka'ris Rudder from East Elmhurst, New York (east of Manhattan) lay down on a set of three seats several rows behind them. He too, had distinguished himself as a starter on both the football and basketball teams after only three and one-half months at the school. Scheduled to take the West Virginia State Certification Program for nursing assistants in April, his long-term goal was to attend college in some field of medicine.

Thomas Loatman of Vienna, Virginia, chose to sit near the back of the car. At 23, he was the oldest of the group. Described by those who knew him as mature, quiet and focused, Loatman had come to the center two and one-half months earlier with a high school diploma and a hope that the Job Corps program could help him acquire the self-discipline that he would need to enroll in a local community college and earn a degree in accounting. His father had phoned the night before and offered to drive up get him, but Thomas insisted on riding the train.

Dante Swain, 18, lived in downtown Baltimore. He had discovered hidden talents during his twenty months on the

Job Corps campus. An athlete and peer-counselor who was consistently on the honor roll, Swain was especially known for his trademark expression, "Boys, let's get it right!" He grew up playing the drums for the Zioneers Gospel Singers back home. His driven interest and chosen profession was carpentry, and he had donated his skilled labor on special projects for the National Park Service during his time in Harpers Ferry. His long-term goal was to secure a local apprenticeship back in Baltimore.

According to staff members, Claudius Kessoon, 20, was another mature and serious student. He, like the others on the train today, had achieved numerous academic awards and served as a mentor in his dormitory. This aspiring brick mason also enjoyed working as one of the school's barbers.

Jimmy Young had been at The Center for only six weeks. He took a seat by himself in the rear of the car across the aisle from Loatman. His father worked for Amtrak at the Washington Terminal Yard and would be waiting to pick up his son there. The father was friends with Jimmy Major, the substitute conductor on the P286 that day, and the three of them had sat down for lunch together in Union Station several months earlier.

MARC commuter trains are arranged in what are called "push-pull" configurations. That allows the crews to run them in either direction without physically turning the trains around. On the trips *out* from Union Station, northeast to Baltimore or northwest to Brunswick, a single diesel locomotive on the front pulls the passenger cars. On the runs *into* Washington, the trains effectively run *backward* with the engine pushing the cars from the rear in a reverse gear. In that mode, the engineer operates the train from inside a small compartment built into the front of the lead passenger coach, similar to what one would see on an urban subway. It is called a cab control car, and was what was leadiang the MARC P286 train toward Washington from Brunswick on Friday, February 16.

Since the return trip was a true express with only one scheduled station stop, both of the conductors, Jim Quillen and Jimmy Major, decided to ride up front in the small engineer's cab-compartment and talk with Ricky Orr. No regulations prohibited this common practice.

Their coach and the two others behind it could accommodate either 107 or 121 passengers. The seats were vinyl upholstered with approximately 22 doubles on one side of the aisle and 22 triples on the other. In the front half of the car, the seats faced forward. In the rear half, they faced in the opposite direction. The aisle was only 20 inches wide, about the same as one would find on an airplane. When a large person met another walking down it toward each other, one had to lean into a seat space to allow the other to pass. The lead coach had an enclosed toilet in the right rear, near the back door.

At the ends of each car, passengers could hit a large rectangular button or a foot-level, "kick plate" to open the pocket-style door and exit the interior out onto an enclosed metal platform. These small enclosed areas at both ends of the cars were called vestibules. From that point a passenger could either continue to walk forward across a two-foot metal plate bridging the connection between the cars into the vestibule of the next car, or exit the train through a door on the right or left. Once the train started its journey, however, the doors to the outside remained locked and could only be opened by a conductor using a pass key.

At the junctions of the cars, the short passageways between their two adjoining vestibules were protected from weather by a rubber neoprene diaphragm in the shape of a thick, (maybe 6" in diameter) round hose that ran up the sides and over the top of the joints in the shape of a large, upside down "U."

Inside his small, forward compartment, Engineer Ricky Orr sat in a spring-loaded jump-seat that folded down from the wall behind him. His "room" was no more than four feet deep and the width of the car. Pocket doors on each side were portals to the outside. The left side of Orr's compartment had no seat. There, another crew member or visiting supervisor might stand if he wanted to talk with the engineer during a trip. Behind the engineer's left shoulder, a third mechanical sliding door (a regular open and close door on some coaches) opened back into the interior of the passenger compartment. It had a fixed window pane.

The operating controls for the engineer's throttle, brakes and reverser were positioned on a shelf-like console at his fingertips. Their functions were linked all the way back through the train's cars to the pushing locomotive within twenty-seven strands of electrical cable wrapped and insulated in a bulk arrangement. That allowed the engineer to operate his trailing engine from a remote location several cars away.

Sitting inside a 135-ton locomotive while it is *pulling* a commuter train, one cannot escape the feeling of calm invincibility. Imagine traveling 80 miles per hour on top of a tractor-trailer truck that is 75 feet long, two stories tall, packed with thousands of bags of cement and fitted with armor plating. The thing is noisy, it shakes, but it is an overwhelming force. If an automobile were to move into its path, the weight of the locomotive alone would destroy it, like a 250 pound man stepping on an empty soda can.

Sitting inside the modest cab-compartment at the other end of a commuter train while it is being pushed from behind is thrilling because the visual image out the front window is one of blissfully gliding on a magic carpet. On the other hand, the experience will keep the first time guest constantly on edge realizing that he is cruising down the tracks only three feet off the ground, sitting in the front of a Volkswagen bus with about a half inch of light-weight alloy metal and a pane of glass between him and eternity. Some veteran railroaders call these egg-shell encased accommodations "suicide cabs."

Rounding a curve at 79 miles per hour toward an upcoming road (grade) crossing, the rider cannot help but focus on the traffic gates coming down, hold his breath and pray that some impatient motorist won't try to bolt across in front of the train. Crossing gates usually start lowering at least twenty seconds before the train arrives. A slow freight will take longer, and a passenger train will blow past sooner. If the gates stay down after the train has passed, the odds are good that another one is coming the other way on the second track - an easy way to die if one is in a hurry.

Although an engineer's ability to operate a passenger train is the same whether he is sitting in the locomotive or cab car, the radical difference comes into play only if his train hits something. The most frightening scenario is the one in which a locomotive and a passenger cab-car collide head on.

When measured from the tracks upward, the bottom of the thick platform that supports the locomotive's diesel engine and alternators sits higher off the rails that the floor of a cab car. If the huge engine and diminutive cab car ever meet with any degree of speed, the different heights will insure that the heavier locomotive with its platform will penetrate the body of the coach and run almost unobstructed through it.

Mismatched weights of head-on colliding trains, even with a locomotive on the front of each one, create a similar result. In the September, 2008, Metrolink disaster near Los Angeles that killed 25, the substantially heavier freight train shoved the Metrolink locomotive backward, halfway through the interior body of the passenger coach behind it. Mechanical engineers in the field of "train-interaction dynamics" warn that these types of events are inevitable if railroads continue to operate "incompatibly-matched" equipment on the same lines.

Eight

The station where the Job Corps students started their journey that afternoon was located in a town which had, for years, supplied the B&O Company with an overwhelming number of loyal and lifelong workers. For many Maryland railroad men, Brunswick was a special home base.

It all started in the mid-1880s, when the B&O decided to find a location for, and build a large rail-yard and shop facility along its main line west of Baltimore where its freight trains coming in from the Western heartland could be classified (separated, sorted and recombined). Also, steam locomotives could not run more than about 100 miles before they needed servicing. Those requirements dictated a site somewhere in Western Maryland or the Eastern Panhandle of West Virginia.

The company finally selected the sleepy village of Berlin, Maryland, scenically located on the north bank of the Potomac River east of Harpers Ferry. Since the 1830s, Berlin's economy had been linked to the Chesapeake and Ohio (C&O) Canal that skirted the community on its route between Georgetown (Washington D.C.) and Cumberland, Maryland. B&O trains had been running along its single-track railroad through the tiny burg for decades without a reason to stop.

The B&O scouts liked the wide expanse of unused bottomland that bordered the town and appeared to be available. Most importantly, the railroad was exempt from paying property taxes in Maryland. Agents used secretive "straw" buyers to purchase the properties along the one-hundred-yard wide by half-mile long swath that lay between the town and the river. The company then began building its new rail yard and shop facility. At the same time it continued to buy additional acreage around and throughout the town.

At the suggestion of the railroad, the municipality of Berlin opted to change its name to Brunswick, keeping its German immigrant heritage, but preventing company mail from going to the other Town of Berlin located on the eastern shore of Maryland (near today's Ocean City). From 1890 to 1905, the B&O created so many new jobs that the number of residents rose from 200 to a booming 4,000.

As if to match the local growth in population, the company then decided to vastly expand its rail yard into a mammoth facility that would accommodate up to 4,000 railroad cars. Their plans included over a hundred short classification tracks, a roundhouse, engine and car repair shops, coaling stations, water towers and ash removal sidings. In the two years from 1906 to 1907, it built the second 4,250-car yard west of town. That made the Brunswick rail-yard complex seven-miles long with 100 miles of internal tracks, the largest such operation in the United States owned by a single company at the time.

Men poured into the area from the surrounding states of Virginia, West Virginia and Pennsylvania. At the same time, the B&O established a Real Estate Improvement Company to help settle and keep the new immigrants. It sold building lots, erected company houses for rent and donated land for public structures, parks and churches. Home construction soon reached numbers unprecedented anywhere in the 175 miles of Maryland between Baltimore and Cumberland. Most of the structures were tidy, two-story, frame residences set close together in rows terraced along the hillsides bordering and facing the Potomac River. Some were ordered as packages from the Sears and Roebuck Company and Montgomery Ward catalogues, brought to town on trains and assembled by local tradesmen.

In 1907 the B&O set about to construct a wooden, four-story building for a Young Men's Christian Association (YMCA) facility between the town and the tracks. It was designed as a crew hotel outfitted with an 88-bed dormitory, dining facility, barber shop, two-lane bowling alley, pool hall, library, laundry and chapel. The structure was very impressive with over 4,000 square feet on each floor.

Railroad men were required to pay their own expenses when they were out on the road, and while most could find overnight lodging along the line for fifty cents a night, that meant bringing your own sheets and bunking with four to six guys in rooms with no heat or shower facilities and a crude toilet downstairs. If a man checked-in late, he had to find his rack with a flashlight so as not to disturb the men sleeping around him. He would go to work the next day just a filthy as he came off the job the night before.

The YMCA was a wonderful alternative that offered spacious, comfortable accommodations with showers, heat and other amenities at reasonable rates. By 1910 the railroad was heavily subsidizing several YMCAs along its route to the west. One of the side benefits of these centers was that their strict and slightly moralistic management style tended to keep the B&O men out of trouble.

Later, the Brunswick "Y" built a three-story annex onto its facility and equipped it as a company hospital. There, a B&O doctor-in-residence treated accident victims from the yard and served as a "doc-in-the-box" for people in the town who needed immediate medical attention.

By the 1920's Brunswick had become a classic textbook example of a one-industry town with strong internal social bonds. Young men followed their fathers into railroad jobs, and neighborhood wives supported each other while their husbands were traveling for extended periods of time.

The Brunswick YMCA (also called the Baltimore and Ohio YMCA) eventually became the grand patron of organized recreational activities. The members of Y's board of directors were selected from the ranks of engineers, firemen, brakemen, conductors, yard foremen, B&O company officials and local businessmen. At the same time, the company carried out its expressed commitment to provide management expertise for the association. In the late 1920s, the superintendent of the Baltimore Division of the B&O concurrently served as the chairman of the Brunswick YMCA board.

The organization's most ambitious project was creating and maintaining local baseball teams. The town had fielded squads in the surrounding Frederick County, Baseball League since 1918, but early in 1926 they agreed to subordinate their program to the better financed YMCA endeavor. That year the board appointed an athletic committee to organize a community league with six teams, one from each of five railroad departments and another from the young men of the town that were not employed by the B&O.

The best players from the league went on to represent the community in the countywide program. Over the next four years this select group played fourteen games a season, won the pennant three times and were narrowly defeated for a fourth. Almost *thirty* years later, in 1959, Brunswick was still fielding an outstanding team. That year they gloriously ended undefeated after 18 outings.

The B&O also organized a 42-member town band staffed by talented railroad employees and their children. They even paid a professional band-leader to drive 25 miles on back roads down from Williamsport, Maryland, to direct them.

Throughout the 1930s and 1940s the company also offered a unique, complimentary service for the families of its workforce. A special passenger-coach self-powered by a gasoline engine and nicknamed the "doodlebug," transported B&O wives and children on weekly shopping excursions to the nearby regional cities of Hagerstown (27 miles away) and Frederick (21 miles).

Even with half the male population of the community working for the railroad, additional men from Cumberland and Baltimore would flood the town during the week for overnight stays. Many of the older ones avoided the crowd at the YMCA, and chose the simple privacy of rooms rented in the homes of local residents. Some shared apartments with other railroaders or stayed in one of the smaller boarding houses.

The company had a "callers" office on the bottom level of the Y building. Employees there would line up the trains and call the railroaders two hours before they were required to report to work. If a man was needed and did not have a phone where he was staying, a boy would walk to his rented room and knock on the door. Sometimes the callers would also canvass the local hangouts looking for men to work "extra-train" assignments.

The railroad crews labored hard at dirty jobs and liked their drink after they got off work. The downtown business district was only four blocks long, but it seemed like there was a bar or liquor store on every corner. The Baltimore men were called "wharf rats" by the locals, and they in turn were dubbed "eel skinners" by the out of town crowd. The "tabbies" were those from the adjoining Cumberland District, gentle country kittens compared to the hard-nosed Baltimore men.

Well aware of the off-hour activities of its working men, the B&O Company convinced Brunswick's elected officials well before 1920 to outlaw the sale of alcohol within the city limits. National Prohibition shut down the stores that had blossomed outside of town. Moonshine operations up and down the nearby Catoctin Mountain range, especially those in the infamous Frog Hollow, however, kept the railroaders well lubricated throughout those years.

Ephraim's liquor store, located in the first block of East Potomac Street until 2001, opened its door the morning of the day that Prohibition was repealed, December 5, 1933. For years since then, the most popular local watering holes have been the Eagle's Club, Darr's Tavern (later named the Whistle Stop), the Metropolitan, or "Met" (now Uncle Willey's) and the Redman's Club. The Moose Lodge and American Legion also break out the bottles for its members.

In the late 1940s, the Brunswick Fire Company used volunteer labor to build a concrete-block engine house with a large auditorium on the second floor. The hall was designed with a professional stage and seating capacity of 500. Over the coming years, the fire company scheduled shows featuring famous entertainers such as Les Brown, Tommy Dorsey, Guy Lombardo, Jimmy Dean and Patsy Cline.

During World War II, the B&O classified over 100,000 freight cars a month in the Brunswick yards. Because of the huge amount of military materials that were switched there, the government designated the town a strategic national security point and arranged to have anti-aircraft guns shipped to and placed on the surrounding hills. Local American Legion Club members trained and remained prepared to man them if enemy planes were reported to be flying up the Potomac River.

The town continued to reflect both the prosperity and later decline of the B&O Railroad. Up into the late 1950s, crowds of local residents flooded the sidewalks and streets on Friday and Saturday nights. The Home Improvement Furniture and Appliances Store, pharmacy, groceries, shoe repair shop and hardware stores, a dairy, restaurants, movie theater, jeweler, news stands, a huge Newberry's five-and-dime with its polished wooden floor, car garages and insurance offices all fronted on Potomac Street. The stately Kaplon's Department Store took up half a city block. Many of the smaller businesses were started by men who were either injured on the job or grew tired of being furloughed by the railroad and never went back.

Postwar inflation and a rise in the B&O's operating costs led the company to reassess its widespread freight facilities. In 1958, it decided to shut down all of its classification functions in Brunswick and move them to facilities in Cumberland, Maryland, and Glenwood, Pennsylvania (near Pittsburgh).

When the Chessie System purchased the B&O fifteen years later, that company moved switching-work back to Brunswick and invested millions in the yard there. With the resurgence of the coal in the 1970s, Brunswick again became the favored location to classify freight cars,

A final reversal of fortune hit the town in 1988 when the railroad's new owner, CSX, decided to close the car repair yards and leave only a skeleton crew at the machine shop. In that year, the number of employees working nationwide on what had constituted the old B&O lines was less than 12,000.

In retrospect, the culture of Brunswick in the first half of the twentieth century proved to be a successful example of labor and industrial-capital working together to the mutual benefit of both. The national economy, with its cyclical phases of over-extension [runaway exuberance] followed by stark recession or new century business plans, however, eventually winnow out some of the best-working, capitalistic models and the locations where they prospered.

Today only a few residents in the town work for CSX. The car-yard operations and the roundhouse are gone. The company sold off all the antique cabooses that had been parked in the yards for years, tore up a hundred miles of track and demolished the roundhouse. All the major repair work on freights is now performed by workers at the high-tech Cumberland shops and the Ivy City facility outside of the Washington, D.C. Terminal yard.

There is not much commercial life left in the former downtown. The facades of the buildings have not changed, but most of the insides are empty or occupied by marginal tenants. The YMCA burned in 1980. A hardware store like the one you remember from your childhood remains open for business on Potomac Street. Uncle Willey's is still there as is the Legion and the fire hall on Potomac Street. The stately churches continue to cast long shadows. Most everything else has been replaced with sleepy antique shops and a couple of classy museums that are well worth seeing. Several years ago a new strip shopping center opened up near the Rt. 340 bypass, about a mile and 70 years away from downtown.

Freights now pass through without stopping like they did in 1880. The remaining train yard with its station on one side and second platform on the other has become a commuter rail hub and parking lot for a hundred-plus people a day. Most of the engineers and conductors operating the freight or MARC commuter trains from here live somewhere else.

Descendants of the old railroad families still occupy the houses on the hills above the town. One of them, Winnie Hane, will tell you, "Regardless of economic ups and downs, Brunswick will always be an island of old-fashioned values and customs. Even today young parents still send their second-grade daughters to school in frilly, starched dresses."

Nine

All across the vast landscape of metropolitan Washington, big flakes of snow were quickly erasing the afternoon sky, and a high wind was moving them sideways. It was one of those "can't wait to get home, build a fire in the fireplace, heat up some chicken noodle soup, watch a little TV and then hunker down under the warm covers and sleep late tomorrow" days.

The MARC crew's official time of arrival in Washington D.C. was 5:50, but with only one scheduled stop and no complications, they usually entered the Union Station terminal about 5:45. On his normal inbound trip, the P286 engineer would see four afternoon passenger trains coming westward toward him out of the city on the left-hand set of parallel tracks. Three of them were MARC commuters and the other was Amtrak's *Capitol Limited*. It usually roared into view at 4:45 near Buck Lodge, approximately 33 miles from D.C.

On that afternoon, however, *The Capitol* was still sitting in Washington, well behind normal schedule. Its two engineers, two conductors, thirteen service personnel and 162 passengers were waiting for Amtrak electricians at the nearby Ivy City shops to repair a defect on one of the train's two locomotives. The engine's smaller alternator, the one that provided electricity for lighting and heating in the passenger coaches (also called HP, or "hotel power"), was not cranking out enough watts.

This historic train had been making roundtrips between Washington and Chicago in different forms under the same name since 1923. For years, its run began in New York, and included Washington on its way to Chicago. Its last trip as the Baltimore & Ohio Railroad Company's signature luxury, long-distance carrier was on May 1, 1971.

It was revived ten years later, in 1981, under the control of Amtrak (an acronym for "American Track") operated by the government-owned National Railroad Passenger Corporation, an organization that, in 2008 alone, transported 28.7 million passengers.

In 1996, the westbound *Capitol,* officially labeled the P029, was scheduled to leave Washington Monday through Friday at 4:05 p.m. Its eastbound counterpart, the P030, regularly departed Chicago later in the evening. They each travel for 19 hours over 765 miles and passed each other early the next morning east of Cleveland, Ohio. En route, the engineers and conductors handed off their trains over to other crews in Pittsburgh, Pennsylvania, and Toledo.

On February 16, Don Noble was designated engineer on the westbound *Capitol.* He commanded that turn on Tuesday and Friday afternoons, and usually arrived in Pittsburgh shortly after 11 p.m. Once they knocked off, the engineers and conductors always took a van to a local hotel around midnight and laid over the entire next day and night.

Throughout the years, the crewmembers succumbed to Noble's affinity for organizing poker games on that day off. Conductor Winnie Hane, often assigned to Noble's Amtrak, liked to say, "He taught me how to lose my money gracefully." In fact, he was a master at the art of bluffing, someone that could often win holding bad cards. That was O.K., Don was both the professional who knew the business of operating

77

their train and a friend who always had time to listen to their opinions.

The group returned to duty twenty-seven hours later at 4:45 a.m. each Thursday and Sunday morning when they relieved the crew bringing the eastbound Amtrak P030 down from Chicago and took it into Washington. With this schedule, Noble, his assistant engineer and two conductors were home three nights a week and enjoyed two, long consecutive days with their families.

Noble was 49 and originally from Westmoreland County, Pennsylvania, just east of Pittsburgh. He, his wife Linda, and their four children had moved from there several years ago to picturesque Middletown, Maryland, a scenic village set on green hills at the foot of South Mountain, forty-eight miles north of Washington. With its unusually tall church steeple and prosperous-looking 1800s homes, the town looks like a scene on a New England calendar. The Nobles purchased some hilly acreage with a large red barn along the historic old National Road.

They initially moved into a local apartment and began overseeing the construction of a new Cape-Cod style home on their "farm." As a skilled carpenter and furniture maker, Don removed some timbers from the barn, planed them for flooring in their new house and crafted some major pieces of furniture. Since he had an ample amount of property, he ventured into landscaping and gardening and briefly experimented with raising sheep.

Like most railroaders, Noble had begun his career working as a brakeman, but after only one year in Pittsburgh, the Baltimore and Ohio selected him in 1978 to enter one of their fast-track engineer-training programs. Nine years later he decided to leave the Chessie (old B&O) System and join Amtrak as one of their regular engineers.

At mid-life, Noble stood six feet tall, was trim in stature and wore a beard and mustache that were starting to go gray from the bottom up. In 1993 he suffered a mild heart attack and began taking two medications and an aspirin each day.

Every summer he and Linda hosted a big party at their home for friends and railroad colleagues. Their usual fare was a bushel or more of steamed Maryland blue crabs cooked with Old Bay seasoning and served with local Silver Queen corn on the cob.

He loved the railroad, was confident in his abilities and particularly enjoyed injecting a good measure of common sense into an occupation where every possible employee action was governed by volumes of company rules. His liberal use of subtle sarcasm and earthy language often left others with the impression that he was cocky and opinionated. But, as a good friend once remarked, "You either loved Don or you really didn't care for him." Most smiled and said, *He is a character.*

His senior conductor, Joseph Richard Ruff, 42, lived in Cumberland, Maryland. Noble liked to coin nicknames for his teammates and called him "Richey." When they were both scheduled to leave out of Washington, Ruff would often drive down from Cumberland to Middletown, park his car in Noble's barn, and the two of them would ride in Don's car to the suburban Shady Grove Metro station. There they would catch the subway to Union Station. Noble often referred to it as the "toy" train.

The assistant engineer that day was thirty-eight-year-old Joseph Fratangelo. "Joey" had been working for the railroad since he was 19. He entered engine service in 1989 as a fireman and was promoted to assistant engineer in 1992. An affable, youthful-looking fellow who got along with everyone, Joey lived in Fredericksburg, Virginia, an hour south of Washington and rode another Amtrak up to D.C. when he was scheduled to serve on *The Capitol.* Friday, the 16th, he was filling in for Kevin Keyes, the regular assistant engineer who had "marked-off," probably because of the weather. Rounding out *The Capitol's* four-man operating crew was David Buffkin, the flagman or junior conductor. His nickname was "Buffy."

Amtrak 29 that day was composed of seventeen units of rolling stock arranged in the following sequence - two diesel-electric locomotives running back to back pulling six "material handling" (mail) cars, one baggage car, one "transition" coach-sleeper for the on-board (or service) staff who traveled all the way to Chicago, two passenger-sleeping cars, a dining car, a sightseer lounge, two regular seats-only coaches and a coach-dormitory unit for the service crew members. With all the passengers, baggage and mail, the "consist" (total composition of the entire train) weighed an impressive 1,436 tons.

The lead locomotive on *The Capitol Limited* was an older model (EMD F-40PH) powered by a two-stroke, twelve-cylinder, diesel engine that generated 3,000 horsepower. These locomotives, called "the workhorses that saved Amtrak," had efficiently and reliably powered the nation's passenger trains for over 25 years. Linked behind the F-40PH that afternoon, was a three-year-old, GE Genesis P40. Its 4,000 "horses" assured that this stunningly powerful team of engines could manage any grade on its trip to Chicago.

While the snow continued to thicken on the ground, Don Noble and his crew sat and waited for the Amtrak electricians to solve the problem on their younger locomotive.

Ten

Crawford Boggs was one of 32 dispatchers working the afternoon shift that day at the CSX Corporation's dispatch center in sunny Jacksonville, Florida. Those were the people who had the job of directing and monitoring 1,400 trains running over 22,000 miles of tracks east of the Mississippi River from a single building formally titled The Kenneth C. Dufford Transportation Center - more widely and popularly called "the bunker." Some railroaders with a unique sense of humor referred to it as "the death star."

Located across the tracks in a deteriorated residential neighborhood west of the downtown, the facility consisted of a block long, two-story, brick structure with all of its ground-story windows sealed shut. A large circular appendage, which a curious passerby might have guessed to be an indoor gymnasium, was attached to its western end. A tall, chain-link fence surrounded the edifice, and the complex looked like a former neighborhood school.

Operations at the bunker began in 1989 when CSX consolidated thirty-four of its existing dispatching sites from around the Eastern United States into this single hub outfitted in Jacksonville, and eliminated over 200 jobs. The new center used state-of-the-art computer software that could follow the progress of all CSX trains, automatically switch crossover tracks and set some signals. It also helped dispatchers identify fast trains that could run around and ahead of slower ones.

When everything was operating normally, a dispatcher could type train identification numbers, tonnages, route speed limits and other vital data into his computer and let the program figure out which ones would go first, last and when. What the system could not do was handle the broken down or delayed ones that could quickly clog up the lines. When that happened, the man had to step in and manually take over the management of traffic in that geographic sector.

Everyone that worked at the bunker was required to present proper identification at the guarded parking-lot gate and two security doors before gaining access to a windowless round-room, about 150 feet wide and two and one-half stories high. The scene inside was actually a huge amphitheater configured into three, round tiers that rose in two-foot increments from the outer ring at ground level to a fourth level in the center. This top, bull's-eye platform contained offices with large interior windows that looked down on the entire operation. It was the domain the general manager, the assistant manager and the Amtrak coordinator.

The train dispatchers sat at large individual consoles spaced around the first and third tiers facing the high outer wall. Mid-level managers sat ahead or behind them on the second level. A few were locomotive technical people, but most were the chiefs. The floors, walls and ceiling throughout the room were covered with materials that kept it almost silent even though a dozen people may be talking at the same time. Audio headsets connected each of the dispatchers via a two-way radio system with individual train crews and other field personnel within their assigned territories, or districts. Shifts were eight hours long with no scheduled breaks. Most of these men and few women did not get out of their chairs during that period.

In 1996, they all had nine-foot-tall, rear projection screen "model boards," conveniently placed on the walls in front of them. These graphic devices displayed the track lines and train locations (lights) in their territories, some of which easily extended up to a couple of hundred miles.

The dispatchers' computer monitors also showed the individual blocks – the one to two mile long subdivisions with signals at each end - that their trains were occupying. Beyond that, the network was not refined enough to let them know whether the trains were at the beginning, middle or end of those zones.

Boggs had been employed at the center for sixteen of his twenty-nine years with the railroad. From 3 to 11 p.m. on Fridays and Saturdays he was the "AU" territory dispatcher (identification call-letters for the geographic area running from Baltimore to Washington to Brunswick). Since he rotated into that particular job only two days a week, he was considered a "relief" man for the AU area. Tuesdays through Thursdays he was the principal dispatcher for another CSX division which did not have any commuter trains. In other words, his forte was dealing with freights.

The AU dispatchers' busiest time was usually between 6 a.m. and 9 p.m. every weekday. During that high volume period (parts of two shifts) they could easily be monitoring and controlling the movement of 80 freight and passenger trains on three different stretches of lines.

Like the others seated around him at the center, the AU man was also responsible for transmitting hard-copies of train orders to each of the crews in his area of authority before they began their runs. These documents not only authorized one or more named conductors and engineer to operate each train, but contained daily lists of temporary restrictions – usually reduced speed limits set in areas where men were out on the tracks performing roadway repairs. In effect, the orders often delayed a train's normal schedule.

The Jacksonville dispatchers were also empowered to remotely operate the signals and switches at traffic control points along their double-track lines called "interlockings." Those are short stretches (usually several hundred feet in length) that have two sets of "crossover" switches that can route trains going in either direction over to the adjacent set of parallel rails. Historically, most of them were located at "junctions" where a branch line intersected the main line.

All of the switches and signals in these interlockings are electronically linked to one another and designed to prevent any human from inappropriately controlling them through "mishap, malice or contrivance." Once the switches have been set by the dispatcher for a train to cross from one of the parallel tracks to the other, or for a train to enter the main line from a branch, all other trains are kept out of the interlocking by red signals on wayside towers.

These interlocking signals are called "absolute" signals because approaching engineers must stop and wait until the dispatcher changes the lights. The system does not allow him to reset them until the train present within the interlocking has passed out of that protected space. Dispatchers occasionally use the absolute block signals to hold trains at one of many designated locations when traffic gets congested.

These short interlockings are spaced from eight to twelve miles apart on the Met Line between Washington and Brunswick. During the peak hours every day, 28 freights, 24 MARC commuters and 2 Amtraks pass through them. Every seasoned engineer will tell you that he always approaches an interlocking with caution. The one that would become infamous this day was, and still is, located eight and one-half miles northwest of Union Station just west of the little brick Silver Spring, Maryland station, *Georgetown Junction*.

Eleven

4:33 p.m.

Rock Runner was the popular name given to the freight that carried crushed quarry stone from Millville, West Virginia near Harpers Ferry, to Bladensburg, Maryland, outside Washington. Every weekday its engine pulled 30 to 35 loaded cars through the Brunswick yards and down the Met line past D.C. In the early afternoons it returned with empties past the entrance to the Washington Terminal Yard and back to Millville.

Because of the weather related problems that Friday, it arrived late to the Washington Terminal bypass track, minutes before the first afternoon Brunswick commuter trains were scheduled to leave Union Station. Dispatcher Boggs quickly decided to keep the freight off the westbound Met tracks until he could get a few of the MARC commuter trains and the Amtrak *Capitol Limited* out ahead of it.

The spot where Boggs held Rock Runner was just outside of an interlocking called QN and named for the nearby Queenstown neighborhood. It was, by far, the most active set of switches on the entire Brunswick/Met Line and at one time years ago had its own individual tower and switch operator. At that critical rail junction, the Jacksonville dispatcher could do several different things with approaching trains.

His three primary options were;

(1) route a train arriving from Brunswick and other points west into the Washington Terminal Yard,

(2) connect a train that was leaving Union Station onto the main line toward Brunswick, and

(3) hold a train that was moving east or west past Washington (like the Rock Runner) until others could exit the terminal yard.

When he had stopped the Rock Runner outside of the QN interlocking, Boggs entered a command into his console to open one of the switches within the QN that would allow an early inbound passenger train from Brunswick (the P284) to enter the branch line leading through the yard to Union Station. Once that train was off the main line, Boggs sent another electronic request to open another QN switch, the one that would allow the first westbound MARC leaving Washington toward Brunswick to move onto the main line Track #1.

His panel light indicated that it did not open.

He tried it again, two, five, ten more times to no avail.

Boggs was silently baffled. This jammed switch at QN could become a big problem. Sitting in balmy Jacksonville, he did not know that the snowfall around Washington had substantially increased since he came on duty, and that its accumulation could easily be the culprit. The dispatcher whom he had relieved two hours earlier had told him about reports of bad weather and added that "switch-heaters" (metal boxes filled with kerosene, fitted with a wick and positioned under all the crossover switches) had been lighted by road crews. Boggs assumed that the heaters were doing their jobs. It was possible, however, that a heavy gust of wind or a passing train had blown a few of them out. Only a local ground crew under the direction of the road-master could find and solve the QN problem.

He called the local dispatcher in Brunswick.

"Doris, could you see if you could get a-hold of Roger Taylor
and tell him I've got switches not working at QN.
[Can he] get somebody out there to clean 'em out?"

Doris acknowledged his request, and Dispatcher Boggs turned his attention back to his looming challenge – how to keep the traffic moving. Since the normal westbound Track #1 was not available for his passenger trains leaving Washington, his most logical alternative was to send them out toward Brunswick on the parallel *inbound* Track #2 and move them back over to the *outbound* Track #1 several miles out at the Georgetown Junction interlockling.

The movable part of a switch (like the ones at QN) is composed of two short sections of rail anchored and hinged on fixed rails at one end and tapered to a slender point at the other, or "free" ends. The dispatcher can electronically make the free ends slide in tandem right and left to open or close the switch. When the device is opened, or "reversed," it routes a train over to another set of tracks. Closed, or "lined up," it keeps the train on the same tracks. In adverse winter weather, however, snow and ice can build in the four-inch gap that separates the tapered points from the adjoining rails and keep them from closing snugly against the those rails when they are electronically directed to do so. If they are not set properly, a train passing over could possibly jump off the rails.

Boggs tested the Georgetown Junction (GJ) switches on his console; open, close, open, close. They worked. At 4:33 he "reversed" his crossover switches there.

For the time being, the westbound Amtrak and MARC trains would leave D.C. on the Track #2 and cross back over to Track #1 when they reached GJ. The signal towers at the west end of GJ all went red. That would prevent any train from entering the space from the northwest. Technically the dispatcher would have trains running toward Georgetown Junction from the east and the west on the same set of rails. The signals, however, according to a hundred plus years of iron-clad railroad procedures, were adequate safeguards to avoid any problems.

Temporarily running trains on the "wrong" set of tracks is a common railroad practice. Dispatchers often do it to move traffic around a temporary blockage such as a disabled train or tracks under repair. An inner city analogy would be to route automobiles up a one-way street the wrong way for a couple of blocks to get them around a broken water main on a parallel one-way street. Traffic coming the right way down the same street, would be intermittently stopped and held.

A Brunswick-to-Washington bound engineer would not only have a red stop signal at GJ, but also a yellow "approach" signal at Kensington (two and one-half miles before GJ). That would instruct him to slow down to 30 miles per hour throughout the entire two and one-half mile block and be prepared to stop at Georgetown Junction.

At 4:38, five minutes after he reversed the switches at GJ, Boggs released the first. westward-bound commuter train out of Union Station. It passed the clogged QN switch and headed toward Brunswick on Track #2.

Within a few minutes of that time, the MARC P286 crew of Orr, Quillen and Major, still far out in the country, were running headlong into a delay only twelve minutes down the road from Brunswick. An insignificant freight train, number Q401, had broken down eleven miles ahead of them and was blocking their track. The text of the warning call from AU dispatcher Boggs to Engineer Orr was picked up on the CSX dispatch center's voice recorder.

Boggs to Orr: "P286, [you] got a man ahead of you before Buck Lodge in emergency (broken down). You might wanna get stopped. I have to get you to back up to Rocks and down #1 track to get you away from there, over."

Orr: "What? You want me to stop?"

Boggs: "Yeah, go ahead and stop if you can."

Orr: "We'll be late."

Boggs: "What did ya say Ricky?"

Orr: "Hey, hey. We're at milepost 41.8" [one mile east of Point of Rocks]. I'm stopping."

Boggs: "Okay, you have permission to reverse back to Rocks, and we'll try to get you around him on #1 track there, over. Did you copy P286? Over."

Orr: "Yes, I copy. We'll go back to Rocks, wait for a signal, and then we'll head east on #1 track."

Boggs: "That's correct, thank you P286."

Boggs was ordering Orr to stop, reverse his engine, back up a mile to just beyond the interlocking at Point of Rocks and wait for the dispatcher to "throw" the crossover switch. Orr could then move over to the parallel tracks and travel back down it to pass the freight. The next crossover point was twelve miles ahead at Buck Lodge. There Boggs would switch the MARC train back across to the #2 track well out in front of the freight. This common maneuver was called a "turndown."

After Orr had stopped his MARC 286, Conductor Jimmy Major walked back into the body of the passenger car to explain the situation to the Job Corps students. A broken-down freight was ahead of them. Their train was going to have to back up about a mile, move over onto the other track and come back down around it.

Senior conductor, Jim Quillen would direct Engineer Orr from the locomotive in the rear using his two-way radio. He grabbed his coat, walked the length of the three coaches, climbed out the rear door of the last one onto the catwalk of the reverse-facing engine, walked around to the front and entered the engineer's compartment. There he could provide "sight" for his engineer back in the cab car.

Orr shifted the directional mode of his locomotive, and with a sudden jolt, the passenger cars started rolling backward. When the P286 had moved past the Point of Rocks crossover, Quillen walked back through the three cars to the cab compartment.

From the bunker in Jacksonville, Boggs reversed the switch and its signal turned to green. Orr started his train through the switch over to #1 track.

Rodney Crawford, one of the Job Corps students, found Conductor Jimmy Major and asked him. "Do you think we'll be late? Me and my buddy are supposed to catch a Greyhound bus near the train station. I think it was at 6 o'clock"

Major replied, "Don't worry, we should make it."

A few of the first-time student riders were nervous about the train backing up and changing tracks and vented their fears by clowning around. Someone called out, "What if we got into a train accident or something?"

Another boy shouted out, "Man, what if we hit another train because we switched tracks?"

Calvin Williams looked over at Tyrai Boyer and whined, "I want to get off. Let me off this train."

Damien reassured the little group around him, "Just calm down. Don't you think they know how to do this? It's their job. Everything is going to be taken care of. It's cool, just calm down."

In the Florida dispatch center, Boggs had taken care of the P286 and his temporary re-routing of outbounds between QN and Georgetown Junction and was turning his attention to other problems. Two passenger trains from Baltimore had been delayed by a malfunctioning switch at Savage and were trying to get into the Washington Yard. Seven freight crews were asking for assistance with signals or orders. In addition, Boggs had five passenger trains scheduled to leave Union Station over the next 40 minutes.

That was far more stress than Boggs normally experienced on his regularly assigned desk. At 5:53 his supervisor called to question him.

"This is Russell Curtis."

"Hey, Curtis."

"I didn't hear anything from you. [...]"

"I got switch failure at QN so I can't get anything over on #1 track. It's derailed (unable to open)."

"They can all go up #2 Track, can't they?"

"Yeah, I got 275 going up through there right now. I also got a problem with... I got an eastbound Q401 in emergency between Buck Lodge and Point of Rock. [...] He's been in emergency three times. I've got P286 up on a turndown. [...] backed-out at Rocks... He's going down #1 track to get around. [...] Then 401 called me and told me he's ready to go again. I told him he's not going anywhere 'till 286 can get by him."

"Jesus Christ."

"I'll tell you. It's everywhere, though. All these damn switches, none of my crossovers want to work. Every time I throw one, I've got to throw it a dozen times to get it to work at all. The one at Savage never would work. [...] I'll tell you if it wasn't for the crossover failures, I would have been okay. [...] So the crossovers are killing me." "I guess with the weather conditions as they are... they say it's snowing and blowing so hard out there they can't keep the pots lit on the switches. [...]"

"I hear ya. All right . . . Maybe we can at least keep these westbound commuters going anyhow. I hope in the next thirty minutes everything will be straight on this [line]."

The students on the MARC P286 watched as their train finally ran past and ahead of the stalled freight.

"Oh there it goes!" someone looking out the window says.

Damien turns to his friend, Eric Garcia and smiles, "G.C. we just switched back onto the right track!."

Garcia replies, "Yeah, that's what it felt like to me too."

"All right, cool man."

The young men relax. Most of them return to napping.

The MARC was once again underway on its trip to Washington. The reverse maneuver, however, had eaten up all of the slack time built into the P286's schedule. With no more delays, it should reach and pass through Georgetown Junction at approximately 5:36.

Twelve

Quillen and Major remained with Engineer Orr in the small cab compartment as their MARC 286 rushed down the road. Since their only scheduled station stop had been at Point of Rocks, they were anticipating an uninterrupted ride with plenty of time to talk. Chances were good that the subject of that conversation was the current and hot labor issue – the CSX roster consolidation.

Most of the long-serving conductors and engineers in the Baltimore Division were seriously upset about it. On the same P286 run the day before, Willis Henry had listened to Quillen and Orr talk about the roster problem all the way back to Washington. This day Quillen and Orr's old friend and union officer, Jimmy Major, was on-board in Henry's place. He would have an interesting assessment of the situation.

Two years earlier, in 1994, CSX had given notice to the unions that it was making a significant personnel policy change. The company's acquisition of three major railroads had not erased the old district lines that still divided those former companies' 1,300 employees into a multitude of fiefdoms spread over a huge area ranging from Southern Virginia north to Philadelphia and west of the Allegheny Mountains.

CSX believed that the numerous labor agreements which still existed within those territories were no longer relevant or valid. Trains passing from one former jurisdiction to another were still required by union contracts to change crews at artificial boundaries even though CSX Corporation legally had consolidated all of the lines. In addition, the unions insisted that employees should not have to compete for local jobs with others from outside of their former districts.

The company's opinion was that such an antiquated system blatantly frustrated management's ability to efficiently allocate its manpower. CSX then decided to take the lead in shaping the outcome of this issue by reinterpreting the many collective bargaining agreements and merging the seniority lists from six districts (including the two around Baltimore that they had owned for years) into one new "Eastern B&O Consolidated Roster."

In theory, that could change the seniority standing of hundreds of conductors and engineers and raise the real possibility that many of them might be forced to physically relocate.

The unions knew that this action might also eliminate some local administrative jobs. Labor attorneys argued that CSX's unilateral alteration of existing contracts violated a long-standing Interstate Commerce Commission (ICC) ruling that protected employees affected by mergers.

Two months before the upcoming 1996 accident, a court-appointed arbitrator issued a binding opinion in favor of CSX. The wording of the ruling satisfied the ICC because it also contained a caveat that CSX must continue to pay full wages and fringe benefits to any displaced employee for six years, even if he or she was not working. The ICC also agreed with the arbitrator's rationale that *seniority status was not a protected right* in the same sense that pay and fringe benefits were. The rosters could be merged.

The unions continued to fight by seeking a "stay of a ruling," but the U.S. Court of Appeals for the District of Columbia Circuit denied their motion on January 5, 1996. Ten days later CSX notified the labor groups that it would implement their new roster consolidation on January 30. The unions reacted with an announcement that they would strike unless CSX rescinded its plans. The company persevered, however, and was successful in their drive to obtain a preliminary injunction from the district court in Baltimore to quash that threat. A final appeal by the unions would not be heard in court until May.

In the meantime, the seniority merger moved forward unimpeded. An announcement of the "preliminary" list (total numbers by job category not a list showing where each man stood in line) came out three days prior to the accident on Tuesday, February 13, and it quickly became the hot topic of conversation among the road crews from that time forward.

Jim Quillen and Jimmy Major both enjoyed superior standing in their pool of 246 Baltimore Division conductors, but it looked like they were about to be shuffled into a new deck of 695, men from other districts who could possibly end up ahead of them on an expanded seniority list. Because of one simple company decision, they might end up losing much of the precious seniority that they had earned over the past 25 years.

Quillen was overwrought that the location of his job may be subject to change. He had just uprooted his family and moved from Baltimore to Frederick, According to a close friend, James Shugars, Quillen was also very worried about his personal financial situation.

Ricky Orr was one of the lower-seniority engineers on the Baltimore District's passenger-service rolls. Even though he had worked many years to secure his current position and higher income, he had not held it that long and could see himself dropping ten or fifteen turns and ending up with a less desirable, disjointed set of daily runs..

With their members pressing hard from one side and the company and courts from the other, the unions compromised. They accepted a new "formula" proposed by CSX. It stated that the sub-division that had the most freight tonnage, Baltimore West, would have the privilege of placing their seven highest-seniority conductors at the top of that territory's turn lists. Three Baltimore-East men could claim the next three turns behind them, followed by two Cumberland guys. Finally, a former Western Maryland Railroad man would round out the first tier. The list would continue downward tier by tier using the same protocol. Engineers would similarly be recorded and ranked based on their subdivisions' historic workloads.

Many of the rank-and-file from the Baltimore Division believed that the United Transportation Union (UTU) and Brotherhood of Railroad Engineers and Trainmen (BLE-T) had not fought hard enough to represent their interests, but had sold them "down the river" by even considering such an idea. It didn't make sense to them. The logical assurances offered by their unions and the courts did not make them feel any more comfortable. To make things worse, the regional union offices that effectively stood to be downsized by the CSX roster seemed to be publicly criticizing the ones that appeared to be unaffected.

Thirteen

A 5 p.m. the Amtrak electricians at Ivy City shops north of the Washington Terminal Yard completed their work repairing the electrical breakdown on *The Capitol Limited.* The source of the problem had been an alternator on the train's newer locomotive, a P40-811 built in 1993. *The Capitol's* other engine, an F-40 locomotive manufactured sixteen years earlier in 1977, was running flawlessly, so the Ivy City technicians recommended that it be used to lead the train on its trip to Pittsburgh. The repaired unit would be placed second in line behind it. The two diesel-electric locomotives were coupled back to back for ease of movement in and around the Washington Terminal yard and would continue in that formation throughout their trip westward.

One of the electricians, Michael French, was assigned to ride in the cab of the second locomotive as far as Harper's Ferry, West Virginia (the first hour) to keep an eye on its shaky electrical system. In railroad terminology, he would be a "mechanical rider."

Although the older, lead locomotive was performing well, it was severely outdated in one respect - its 1,800 gallons of diesel fuel would be carried in what is called a "non-compartmentalized" tank (one big container with no interior partitions). The National Association of American Railroads had recently and strongly recommended that these types of tanks immediately be replaced with new "fuel-cell" (multiple-compartment) models that were mandated for all units manufactured after 1995. A rupture in the wall of one of the newer tanks would release only a small portion of the stored diesel fuel, not most of it like the older tanks would. Amtrak had not followed up on that advisory to retrofit. The more recently manufactured second locomotive, however, *was* equipped with one of the safer tanks.

The concept of the diesel engine was patented in 1892 by a German citizen, Dr. Rudolph Diesel, who lived in both that country and France. At the time, he was a 34-year-old thermal engineer who was working on inventive methods to refrigerate beer. One of his employer company's larger clients was the American Anheuser Busch Brewery in St. Louis. Diesel's driving personal ambition, on the other hand, was to invent a combustion engine that could operate efficiently using inexpensive vegetable oils derived from commodities such as peanuts, corn, sugar cane and soybeans. Over a period of five years he fabricated a working, compressed-air model and later demonstrated it at the 1900 World Exposition in Paris using *peanut oil* as fuel!

The traditional internal-combustion engine uses what is called "spark ignition," a vaporized mixture of gasoline and air injected into small chambers where it is ignited by electric sparks to start and continue to run the engine.. The mini-explosions move pistons and rotate the engine's driveshaft.

With Diesel's invention, air alone first would be injected into his engine's combustion chambers and *compressed* to a point at which its temperature would rise into the range of 1300 to 1650 degrees Fahrenheit. When liquid vegetable fuel was sprayed into the same compartments, it would ignite with an explosive force similar to that created by gasoline. Diesel's "compression-ignition" thermal engine was based on the principle that one needed extra-high temperatures to ignite liquid fuels extracted from plant materials.

The idea of producing vegetable oils as a primary fuel was forgotten years before the inventor died in 1913. Variations of his engine began operating with the most popular fuel of the day, crude kerosene, and those engines were built to run huge generators that cranked-out inexpensive electric power for major cities.

What later came to be known as "diesel" fuel (which Rudolph did not invent) soon replaced kerosene as the power source for his engines. Petroleum diesel has been described as a waste product derived from the process of refining gasoline and home heating oil. It worked perfectly in his new engines because it required higher temperatures to ignite. One of the fuel's redeeming features was that it produced 18% more energy per unit of volume than gasoline. That translated into a 20% to 30% increase in fuel efficiency.

While Diesel was living, the U.S. military began actively contemplating using his engines in its land vehicles, but the railroad industry did not begin to recognize the value of Diesel's invention until the early 1930s.

Railroad mechanical engineers eventually adopted the concept of the diesel engine, and they modified it into a hybrid arrangement called the "diesel-electric" locomotive. This innovation followed the same two-part principle that the electric-power companies had been using for years, conversion of mechanical energy from diesel fueled engines rotating shafts on generators into electric power produced by those generators.

That is how it continues to work today. A locomotive's diesel engine turns a crankshaft that extends back into the heart of a large, on-board alternator. As the shaft spins, the alternator produces enough electric current to service about 1,000 homes and that juice is routed downward to four individual electric motors, one wrapped around each of the locomotive's four wheel axles. These so called "traction motors" are the instruments that actually turn the wheels and pull (or push) the train. They can smoothly accelerate the locomotive from a standstill to full running speed without the use of the 15 gears that would be required if the diesel engine itself was harnessed directly to the wheels.

An engineer changes his train's speed by moving the throttle laterally through ten separate positions. "Stop" is followed by "idle" and increasing speed settings (1 through 8). While each of these "running notches" slightly elevates the spin of the shaft in the engine and alternator, it primarily regulates the rotational speed of the traction motors by increasing, or reducing, the amount of current that passes down to them.

Today's "innovative" hybrid automobiles use some of that same historic technology. A hybrid vehicle contains a gasoline engine that can charge an attached alternator. The alternator sends electricity into a battery which, in turn, directs current to an electric motor that turns the automobile's axles and wheels. When the batteries need recharging, the gasoline engine is able to do that as well as temporarily power the car by itself. In 2009 Volvo announced that it will produce a *diesel-electric* automobile by 2012.

In the Depression year of 1935, the Electro-Motive Division (EMD) of the General Motors Corporation built the first diesel-electric locomotives in the United States for switching cars in rail yards. From that point they moved directly into the design of others that could pull trains over long distances and compete with steam engines.

The big limiting factor surrounding steam engines was always the fact that only one could effectively move a train.

Two were sometimes lashed together, but that linkage (a doubleheader) often proved to be difficult to operate with two separate crews on two separate engines. Two in front and one in back was an arrangement that was sometimes employed to temporarily get a heavy train up a steep grade, but longer freights running over normal lines always required larger and more powerful locomotives. Companies like the Baldwin Locomotive Works of Philadelphia built marvelous and beautiful monsters that are now housed in museums such as the Smithsonian in Washington. Their sizes, however, soon reached the limits of the tracks to safely handle them.

The ultimate success of the diesel-electric models was the workable idea that they could be built smaller and coupled together to substantially increase their individual pulling power. At the same time, the running electrical commands from the lead locomotive were designed to be transmitted through a strand of wires from the first engine to the last. These "multiple-unit" controls allowed a single engineer to operate all of them in tandem. That significantly expanded the power available to pull any payload within existing track specifications. By 1939, the EMD had successfully attacked steam's last stronghold, main line freight.

The diesel locomotives hit the ground operating with a "mechanical efficiency" of 75.6 percent. Steamers, even the larger ones that generated over 4,000 horsepower, historically ran at 10 percent. Ninety percent of their generated power was lost into the atmosphere. With few moving parts to wear out, the diesels also could travel non-stop over 600 miles without being serviced. That was six times further than its coal-fired predecessors.

In spite of the fact that these new-technology locomotives proved to be expensive, the railroads soon began to embrace them because of their long-term financial benefits. Companies no longer needed to buy different-sized steam engines to pull their cargoes across the plains and over mountain ranges. Running a steam train at 60 to 80 m.p.h. and keeping it at that speed required the highly refined mechanical skills and muscular prowess of at least two strong men. The fireman alone would shovel and rake up to 12 tons of coal in his firebox over a 12-hour day. With diesel engines, a solitary man could comfortably operate two, four, or more locomotives linked together and move the load behind him up any hill, "making the grade," without losing power.

The big savings for the companies did not come from the elimination of firemen, but the "reorganization" of the rest of the workforce. Well over fifty percent of the tens of thousands of steam-era skilled workers; machinists, boilermakers and metal-smiths who labored in company back-shops fabricating worn-out or damaged parts were gently phased out because diesel locomotives used standardized parts which could be quickly shipped by manufacturers. Water-tower operators, coal loaders, ash removal people and fire-box re-builders were all about to become toast. The conversion to diesel power was complete by the mid-1950s.

Since the diesel engine is only needed to create electric current (via the on-board alternator), the presence of overhead electric lines along some urban railroad corridors such as the Amtrak Northeast Corridor between Washington, New York and Boston, eliminated the need for a diesel motor on trains running over those lines. This "straight electric" source of energy is tapped through a hinged arm on top of the locomotive as it moves down the tracks and produces 65% more electric power than the diesel engine could by itself. Unfortunately, the United States (unlike Europe) has very few railroad miles that are served by overhead electric. The Northeast-Corridor railroad power lines used today was originally installed by President Roosevelt's WPA in the 1930s.

Today's locomotive cab, like the ones in the past, contains two seats, the one on the right side for the engineer and the left one for either a freight conductor or assistant engineer. MARC commuter trains use only one man. Because they travel longer distances, the Amtrak trains have always had two.

The engineer's controls are positioned on two vertical walls called control stands or consoles. The one beneath the forward window has handles that regulate the diesel engine and its traction motors. The three major levers are; (1) the locomotive throttle, (2) the dynamic brake, and (3) the reverser. Each one can be operated with the right hand.

The throttle has a "stove pot" handle that protrudes out of the panel. The dynamic brake control, used to regulate the amount of electricity going to the traction motors and slow the train, looks similar and emerges from the wall above the throttle. The reverser is a switch which can change the train's direction (forward and reverse). It is located beneath the other two and is operated by a large, removable brass or hard plastic key. Once the engineer removes that key, the locomotive cannot be moved even if the engine is running.

The two big handles to the engineer's left can engage most of his train's braking-capacity. The red-colored one higher up operates the automatic air-brake system. It has six horizontal positions ranging from the extremes of "brakes totally off" to full emergency (all brakes on). The lower handle controls the locomotive's "independent," or engine-brake.

The interior of the dated locomotive cabs are cold, gray metal - utilitarian and Spartan. A three-step stairwell in the front between the seats leads down to a no-frills, primitive commode and a small, front door exit.

The large diesel engine and main alternator that rest in the room back behind the engineer are less than 15 percent of the locomotive's total weight. The bulk of the remaining tonnage is concentrated in the thick steel floor, or "ballast platform," that they sit upon. It provides enhanced track adhesion and help the locomotive hold the curves at high speeds.

Large front and rear posts inside the locomotive extend downward through that platform to hold two massive wheel devices called "trucks." Each has two axles with fixed wheels on their tips (four wheels total per truck). All the axles are fitted in their centers with wrap-around traction motors which turn them. As the train moves around curves or through crossover switches, the trucks pivot, or swivel, on the posts to smoothly negotiate the directional changes. The freight or passenger cars that follow the engine have similar wheel assemblies on posts, but no traction motors.

Older model Amtrak and MARC locomotives also have the enormous 1,800 gallon diesel fuel tanks that were previously mentioned. They are attached to the underside of the ballast platform and hang between the locomotive's two wheel trucks. Their bottoms ride only *four* inches above the rails. A typical locomotive pulling a passenger train will consume 105 gallons an hour running at 70 m.p.h. (one and a half gallons per mile).

Wheel trucks, the weight of the full-sized locomotive and the non-compartmentalized fuel tank will all soon craft the stunning details of the major event ahead.

When an engineer is preparing for a run, he or a yard "hostler" will climb up an eight-foot ladder on the side of the locomotive and enter its cab. Next he will open a door in the back of the interior cab and step into a tight, confining corridor. There he will engage a knife switch that connects the batteries to the starter circuit, and flip a wall of individual breaker switches that will provide power for everything from lights to a fuel pump.

Stepping further down the small corridor into the engine room, he will turn and holds another switch that primes the fuel system (a choke). Moving that switch the other way, he engages the starter motor. As the engine cranks and begins to run, the engineer will return to the cab to monitor the gauges and set the brakes.

Since the MARC commuters are alternately operated from either end, the engineer may begin his trip from inside the full-sized locomotive or the diminutive cab car compartment at the other end of his passenger train. Once the senior conductor gives him permission to start moving, he assumes a span-of-control that includes moving the train safely forward or backward at different speeds, bringing it to a stop, maintaining air-brake pressure and keeping mechanical and electrical systems running at peak efficiency.

These tasks may seem simple since he doesn't have to steer. But in reality, a passenger train engineer must be able to constantly and accurately align his cars alongside many different platforms while moving hundreds of tons of rolling danger into or out of a sea of sleepy customers milling around the tracks (often in the dark). He quickly develops what are called "train-handling" skills. These are refined and precise movements of both hands over a multitude of handles with the skill of a concert pianist

Notch the throttle up to six; bring it down to two. Apply some air brake, suppress it. Twenty pounds? Maybe a little more. Touch the independent brake. Remember, the orders said there is a restricted speed between the next few mile posts. Signal is at the end of this stretch; can't quite make it out yet. Verbally call that signal on the radio. Grade crossing is coming up. Blow the whistle – long. . .long. . .short. . . . long. Conductor is talking on the radio. What did he say? Station stop is around the next curve. Start applying the air brakes against the throttle. Maybe shift to idle and use dynamic and engine braking for a smoother stop. Don't jerk the passengers. Watch that lady crossing the tracks. Where is my mark to line the cars up with the platform?
Ease it down. Ease it down. . . .
STOP.

Fourteen

Inside the whirlwind of controversy that later whispered and shouted conflicting opinions about the causes of the event that winter afternoon in 1996, no subject was more intensely discussed than the operation of wayside signals.

It has always been possible to run trains safely without signals. Over half of the route-miles in the United States still do not have any. Most of those miles, however, are single-track branches that can only be occupied by one train at a time.

The evolution of signal technology for high-volume rail arteries was initially driven by monetary considerations; safety concerns came in a distant second. In the mid-1800s, railroads used what was called the "time-interval" system to create spaces between their trains running in the same direction. It permitted an engineer to run at full throttle only after the train ahead of his had a full ten-minute head start, or "headway." Signalmen located along the line (usually at stations) used colored flags to tell the engineers how fast they could proceed.

They displayed a red (stop) flag for the first five minutes after a train had passed, and then put up a yellow banner for the next five. That meant that the following train had to move at a reduced speed. When ten minutes had elapsed, the signal man would bring out the green, or "high ball," flag. That indicated full speed.

This primitive system was based on the assumption that all trains would run at consistent speeds and maintain adequate spacing. The locomotives at the time, however, were less reliable than they were later and often were forced to stop in the middle of nowhere. Out-of-sight communications between train crews existed only in the forms of illuminating flares, lanterns and explosive sound devices. If a train encountered a problem and had to stop, a flagman would be dispatched by the conductor to run back up the line to behind it to warn the next one that might be coming. Even if the following engineer was alerted to the presence of a disabled, or blocked, train in front of him, he often did not have enough stopping warning or distance to avoid slamming into it.

The railroads soon discovered a more serious problem with the three-flag arrangement; it seriously limited their line capacity. Ten-minute intervals restricted the number of trains that could run through a geographic sector over the course of one hour. That was a revenue issue. The companies gradually began reducing their margins of headway to run more trains over their lines in less time, and the number of accidents increased. In 1875 alone, over 1,200 railroad employees and passengers died in numerous rear-end collisions.

A concept called "fixed signaling" eventually addressed those problems by chopping up the line into one- to two-mile divisions of track called "blocks," protecting them with mechanical signals at each end and mandating that only one train at a time could occupy the space between. The railroads implemented this "space-interval" system by placing crude mechanical signal devices at both ends of these subdivisions and locating employees in nearby "block houses" to control the oncoming traffic. As soon as one of these men allowed a train to enter his block, he set a red signal behind it and notified the next block man by telegraph that the train would soon be in his territory.

The business-minded rail managers continued to encourage any innovations that would allow them to move higher volumes of freight cars in shorter periods of time using fewer employees. The next technological advancement to increase line capacity and also eliminate block-house employees was invented by Dr. William Robinson in 1872. It was called "automatic block" signaling.

Robinson came up with the ingenious idea of running a low-voltage electric circuit through the rails within each block and connecting it to nearby signal towers. When a train entered a block, its wheels would short circuit (interrupt the flow of current) and cause the signals at both ends of the section to show red lights. This technology was considered "fail-safe" because each block was also electrically insulated from the ones that adjoined it. If connection wires failed, a signal bulb burned out, or a rail broke, the relay would not pick up the current and the tower lights would go blank. That was called a "false signal" and meant that an approaching engineer must stop and move cautiously forward until he could find a working signal.

The only flaw in early automatic block signaling was that an engineer could not begin to react until he saw either the red or blank light. That often did not allow him enough time to bring his train to a complete stop before it rolled well into the restricted zone.

A later refinement established "distant" signals, a concept that is still in use today. Each block was wired in a loop to the ones adjoining it on either side and presented an arriving engineer with a yellow light at the entrance to the block several miles ahead of and behind the one that had a red stop light. This yellow, "approach," signal meant that he must move slowly through the block and remain prepared to stop at the next signal. By the time the engineer arrived at that next signal, it may have turned from red to yellow or even green. But he would not know until he got there.

On the Brunswick Line in 1996, the B&O "wayside" signal towers beside the track were traditional, thirty-foot-tall metal masts topped with large, round disks. Those circular signs had colored-glass lenses arrayed around their perimeters like numbers on a clock. Each lens was eight inches in diameter and was illuminated from behind by a powerful, bright bulb. Individual signal-aspects consisted of two lights of the same color with a smaller, white "pilot" light above or below the large disk.

The two railroad terms used to describe signals are *aspects* and *indications*. Aspects are the colors and configurations of the lights on the signal tower (what the engineers see) and indications are what the lights mean - the speed limits an engineer must observe on his way to the next signal. The other twenty plus signals are slight variations of the three most basic red-stop, yellow-slow and green–go.

In early morning or late afternoon sunlight – the yellow approach lights sometimes appear to be turned off under the reflection of low-angle sunlight. An engineer often has to cautiously creep his train up to such a signal before he can clearly decipher it.

One of the major problems that engineers in commuter service always have to fight on a daily basis is mind-numbing redundancy. Yesterday's block signals blur into today's block signals once they pass them. Some on the Brunswick and Camden line engineers have invented little practices to prompt their memories while they are traveling through a restricted block. For example, one might place a pen or pencil between his teeth after passing a yellow signal to remind him to continue at a reduced speed after he has made an interim station stop.

At the same time, each station stop always has the potential for sudden surprises. Commuters arrive late and do crazy things like sprinting across the tracks in front of an approaching train. It is relatively easy for the engineer to focus on the immediate complication and mentally set aside the aspect of the last signal.

Two additional psychological factors are also working against that same engineer to lull him into a warm sense of complacency. The first, based on experience, is the mind game of assuming that everything is normal ahead and being right 99 percent of the time. The second is overestimating one's ability to react quickly and correctly to the sudden and unexpected.

Most often, a yellow signal will be followed two miles later by another yellow or even a green signal. That norm tends to strengthen the engineer's expectation that it will always be the same. Coupled with that is the seduction that comes with operating a light commuter train. A three-to-six car MARC train, compared to a freight, can be stopped over a relatively short length of track. The commuter passenger engineer must constantly suppress the feeling that he can react successfully within his line of sight.

Indeed, the most famous engineer in railroad history was thirty-six-year-old John Luther Jones, a flamboyant young man who constantly relied on his instincts to predict what was waiting for him around the next curve and his train-handling skills to overcome any delays and meet scheduled arrival times.

The final display of his prowess was recounted in a story that unfolded in the early-morning darkness of April 30, 1900, along the Illinois Central Line running the Delta between Memphis, Tennessee, and Canton, Mississippi. John Luther was not scheduled to operate the prestigious "Cannonball" passenger and mail train #1 out of Memphis that night, but its regular engineer, Joe Lewis, became ill, and the railroad supervisors were desperate for a substitute. Jones, with ten years of operating experience but only sixty days of that in passenger service on the line through central Mississippi, volunteered. His faithful fireman, Simon Webb, agreed to accompany him even though the two of them had just completed a long shift bringing a freight train 188 miles north from Canton.

It was close to midnight when the Memphis dispatcher finally gave Jones and conductor, J.C. Turner, permission to leave the station. They started southward an hour and thirty-five minutes behind schedule. Over the first hundred miles, Engineer Jones and Fireman Webb managed to shave a full sixty minutes off of that deficit.

Shortly after three o'clock in the morning, however, they were signaled to stop in Goodman, Mississippi, and wait for a northbound freight to move out of their way onto a siding. Even with that delay, Jones made it a personal challenge to complete the run on time. Fifteen miles down the road, not far from his ultimate destination, he and Webb were unaware of another complication that was brewing ahead of them.

At the small switching junction of Vaughan, the local dispatcher was feverously working to clear the way for Jones' Cannonball and another express running ahead of it. After he had moved two slow freights onto a north/south siding that paralleled the main line, he discovered that the combined length of the trains was too long to fit onto it. Several cars from had to remain dangling out on the main tracks.

Dispatchers at the time customarily resolved such a problem by ordering a "saw by," a two-staged maneuver that shifted the sidelined trains backward and forward to allow the priority train on the main line to slowly move past them. The first express approaching from the north (the one ahead of Jones) was signaled to slow down, ease up alongside the two freights on the nearby siding, and wait while those nose-to-nose freights rolled their excess cars from in front of him back northward out onto the line behind him. This cleared the rails in front of the express.

The dispatcher then ordered the two freights to move back southward to again open the north end of the main line for the oncoming Cannonball. At that point, either an air hose or a drawbar on one of the freights broke and stopped the move. Several cars remained stranded out on the main tracks north of the siding. The dispatcher knew he had a very serious problem and directed Flagman John Newberry to run half a mile up the line to a point beyond the long curve that led into the junction. His mission was to warn the Cannonball by placing exploding "torpedoes" on the rails and then continue hustling another 800 feet further to a spot where he clearly could be seen waving red and white lanterns.

Although it was later estimated that Engineer Jones and Fireman Webb could see Newberry's signals for a distance of at least a mile, the Cannonball blew past him without slowing down. Webb later testified that the two of them were talking about the new whistle that had been installed on their engine and laughing at how "they would rouse the people of Canton" when they arrived in town. Their train was traveling over 70 miles per hour when its wheels set off the torpedoes.

John Luther then activated his emergency brakes, but his express had only slowed down to only 50 miles per hour when it rounded the curve leading into the station. Jones and Webb were shocked by the scene ahead — red lights on the rear of a caboose blocking the tracks in front of them. Both knew that they were not going to be able to stop in time. Webb panicked and made the decision to leap off the locomotive.

Even though there was nothing else he could do to slow his train once its emergency brakes had been set, Jones stayed at his controls, hoping that he might be able to survive. Fifteen seconds from impact he put the train into reverse.

That did not help him. His locomotive slammed into the rear of the idle freight at 35 miles per hour, compressing the first few cars and blasting wood and steel fragments for fifty yards down the tracks.

In the end, he was the only person killed and would have been just another rail-accident statistic had it not been for Wallace Saunders, an "engine wiper" (engine cleaner) who worked in the Canton shops. Saunders was quite talented and later wrote a catchy little song about the wreck. An engineer friend of his passed it on to his two Vaudeville performing brothers. They brushed up the lyrics, added a chorus and took it on the circuit with them.

John Luther Jones, originally from Cayce, Kentucky, and nicknamed Cayce, or "Casey," Jones at an early age, went down in history as an American hero.

On April 30, 1900, that rainy morn,
Down in Mississippi near the town of Vaughan,
Traveling 50 miles an hour when they saw a freight.
Sped the Cannonball Special only two minutes late,
At 3:52 that morning came the fateful end.
Casey took his farewell trip to the Promised Land.

In a surviving company report, Illinois Central Railroad officials noted that Fireman Webb was awarded a whooping $5 in compensation for injuries suffered as a result of jumping off a train traveling at 40 miles per hour. The two postal clerks on the Cannonball who were "jarred" in the accident each received checks for $1.

In 1950 the Postal Service issued a commemorative stamp to "Honor America's Railroad Engineers" by displaying an engraved portrait of Casey Jones. Since then, the small Town of Vaughan, Mississippi has opened a museum to memorialize his life. Somehow, however, his macho recklessness was re-interpreted over the years as "heroic" simply because he died.

Later, working engineers began using the phrase "a real Casey Jones" to subtly insult one of their own whom they thought was acting cocky and over confidant.

Today, many railroads install "cab signaling" systems with components in both the locomotives and along the tracks. When an engineer passes yellow lights, the most basic form of this technology continues to remind him throughout the block that he is operating under a "slow down" signal. These devices actually date back to 1910 when they were first widely used by the safety-conscious Pennsylvania Railroad.

Transmitters linked to the trackside signal towers are placed in metal boxes between the rails (or overhead) at the block entrances. As a train passes over or under them, the status of the nearby signal is electronically sent to a receiver in the locomotive or cab car. Some versions of cab signaling will sound an alarm if the signal is restrictive. The engineer is then required to acknowledge the warning by hitting a button. Throughout the block he can see, on his console, a visual reminder of the lights behind him. This extraordinary safety device will reinforce the engineer's memory if his attention is diverted by something such as a station stop, and would have prevented what was coming.

The MARC locomotives and cab cars operating on the lines throughout the Baltimore Division from Baltimore to Washington to Brunswick are equipped with "four-aspect" cab signals. These inform the engineer that he is running under one of the following speed directives:

(1) "clear"- normal maximum authorized speed limit,
(2) "approach medium" - generally 45 m.p.h.,
(3) "approach" - 30 m.p.h., and
(4) "restricting" – 15 m.p.h. and expect an impediment ahead
    (another train on your track or switch thrown against you).

Only trains running the Penn Line (former Pennsylvania Railroad tracks) between Washington and points northeast of Baltimore, however, can use the cab signals because that stretch has corresponding electronic hardware installed "in the ground" along the route. The Brunswick and Camden routes do not have the same trackside infrastructure, so their locomotive cab signals are useless.

All train lines, however, are equipped with another type of electronic hardware, "audible defect detectors." Embedded between the crossties or beside the tracks at 20-mile intervals, these warning devices use infra-red beams to pick up signs of overheated wheel bearings, or "hot boxes." Whenever a train moves past or over one of them, the detector will send a human-sounding, voice message to the train crew over their radios, alerting them that their cars are being electronically inspected. Seconds later the same voice announces the results of the scan, problem or no problem.

During that fifteen-second report, however, the conductors and engineer cannot use their radios to communicate either with each other or anyone else up and down the line. The readout is transmitted on the same frequency and effectively blocks all human conversation.

For those fifteen seconds on the 16th of February, this simple safety tool would prove to be an accident accomplice in disguise.

Fifteen

Union Station, Washington, D.C.

Every weekday afternoon, eight to ten passenger trains line up alongside elevated concrete platforms in the rear of this grand building on Capitol Hill. Around 4:20, commuters begin rising up on escalators from the metro subway beneath the building, bypass the glitz of the shops and restaurants and walk directly out onto the platforms. A few of them make a quick detour through the little package store to pick up a carry-out beer, or a half-pint of liquor in a paper sack. The loud whine of idling diesel engines reverberate off the floor of the parking garage above, and clouds of black smoke turn downward into the faces of women and men trying to find their MARC or RF&P (Richmond, Fredericksburg and Potomac) coaches.

By the 1890s, most of the railroads serving major U.S. cities were operating their own terminals in different parts of town. The rapidly approaching mark of the twentieth century, however, inspired railroad executives to begin cooperating with their competitors to consolidate their awkward array of passenger stations and depots into one new architectural

116

masterpiece. As each new "union" station was completed, it was touted to be either the largest or the most beautiful in the world.

Perched on the Northwest corner of Capitol Hill two blocks from the Senate Office Building, Washington's Union Station was constructed as a joint venture by the Baltimore and Ohio and the Pennsylvania Railroad companies. Completed in 1908, it immediately trumped the grand, Romanesque Union Station in St. Louis as the superior-sized monolith of the day. Actually, it was the largest train station in the world and covered more ground than any other building in the United States at the time. The main hall was so wide that the Washington Monument could have been laid on its side within it.

Well into the 1940s, this pride of the nation's capital employed a staff that exceeded 5,000 and offered such amenities and services as a bowling alley, YMCA, bakery, butcher's shop, luxury hotel with presidential suite, ice house, liquor store, Turkish baths, restaurants, floral nursery, police station and mortuary.

Twenty years later, however, the building was well on its way to mirroring the decline of passenger-rail service by slowly deteriorating into several acres of dreary, and smelly waiting-rooms languishing under a rotting, leaky roof. It had become a non-functional albatross, too expensive to fix and too important to tear down. An idea to rehabilitate it into a national visitors' center for the upcoming bicentennial took off, and flopped.

Then, in 1976, Congress and President Ford created the federal tax credit for historic preservation, and that financial incentive, coupled with the concept of public-private partnerships, triggered an avalanche of "festival market," commercial redevelopment projects. The "adaptive reuse" of historic buildings became the stock and trade of many talented development teams over the next decade. In 1988, the Union Station Redevelopment Corporation unveiled its $16,000,000 wonder, a meticulously restored building designed to operate as a high-end shopping mall with restaurants, theaters, a multi-story parking garage and an old-fashioned passenger train terminal with 21 receiving tracks..

Today the complex showcases 130 small and medium-sized stores, an extensive food court, five restaurants, a nine screen cinema and management offices. As it is located next door to the Smithsonian's National Postal Museum and three blocks from the U.S. Capitol building, the facility attracts more than 30 million visitors a year.

5:05 p.m.

Geraldine Audrey Dykes was in her mid-fifties and lived in downtown Laurel, Maryland, one of the stops on the MARC Camden line to Baltimore. She had been commuting from there into Washington for six years. At 5:05 p.m. on Friday the 16th, she walked out onto the rear concourse of Union Station in search of her 5:12 MARC train, strolled down the correct platform and she mistakenly turned right instead of left and boarded the 5:10 to Brunswick instead of the 5:12 to Baltimore. The cars always look the same.

Dykes immediately noticed that the conductors inside didn't look familiar but dismissed the thought with the rationalization that the regular guys had probably taken the day off with the upcoming holiday weekend. She liked to read while she traveled and was soon comfortably seated and absorbed in her current paperback novel.

This Brunswick-bound MARC train eased out of Union Station on-time at 5:10 with thirty-year veteran engineer Jobe Breeden at its controls. When he reached the QN interlocking just north of the yard, his train joined the main line on Track

#2. As he approached each signal heading west, Breeden, like all other engineers operating in the Baltimore and Cumberland districts, was required to activate his radio and verbally "call" what he saw ahead. According to the rule, that included the identification number of his train, the direction it was traveling, the track number (#1 or #2), the milepost and the name and aspect of the signal (every signal location has a name). One of his conductors then was required to affirm his call.

Engineer Breeden: "P279 at milepost 6.3, Takoma Park, heading west on track number 2, with a medium-clear signal."

Conductor; "Roger, P279, medium-clear, I copy you."

Sixteen

The locomotives for Don Noble's *Capitol Limited* were finally brought from the Ivy City shops to the back of Union Station and coupled to the waiting Amtrak coaches and cars. The 164 passengers began walking out onto the platform. Two conductors and fourteen service personal (coach attendants) pleasantly directed those with sleeping-car reservations and regular coach tickets to their cars.

The travelers were predominantly elderly people and young women with small children. Everyone had one or two pieces of luggage. This was not the daily, suit-and-tie, Washington-to-New-York business crowd that rides the Amtrak Metroliner and Acela with briefcases and laptop computers.

Inside, *The Capitol* looked like the most comfortable means of public transportation imaginable. Coach seats were roomy and cushy. One could walk to an observation car, sit in a swivel seat facing window walls and watch the scenery. The café brimmed with snacks and beverages. Downstairs, an isolated smoking parlor attracted a mix of friendly souls amenable to exchanging personal anecdotes. Once the train was underway, a uniformed steward would come around to take reservations and menu selections for one of the two dinner seatings in the dining car.

Engineer Noble had already met with his assistant engineer and conductors in the small metal shack near Track #7 called the Washington Terminal crew office. There the men viewed the Jacksonville Dispatcher's Bulletin, or train orders. This paper printout, running anywhere from two to four pages, was usually a list of temporary, restricted speed limits along their route. Periodically, it also warns the train crews about ground crews that are out there working on the lines ahead of them.

Walking across the back of the station and out the platform to his fifteen-car train, Noble and his senior conductor, Joe Ruff, reviewed the relative positions of the passenger coaches to decide which ones (numbers 12 through 15 back from the engines) they must align with the short platforms at their first few scheduled station stops - Rockville, Harpers Ferry and Martinsburg. The task this day had been made slightly more complicated because the Washington Terminal people had placed seven mail and baggage cars at the head-end of the train. With that arrangement, the engineer could not see any of the passenger cars from the locomotive and had to rely on his conductors to tell him (over the two-way radio) when to stop.

The assistant conductor, Dave Buffkin, walked to the rear of *The Capitol* as Noble climbed up into the cab of the lead locomotive. His assistant engineer, Joey Fratangelo, was already seated on the left-hand side. Buffkin called to them on his radio from beside the last coach; he was ready for the air-brake test.

Noble released the brakes, that move also recharged the compressed-air reservoirs up and down the entire train..

Buffkin watched the brake pads at the end of the last car pull away from the wheels and notified Noble over the radio, "OK, P-029, *apply* brakes."

Noble moved the air-brake handle to "full application." The brakes emitted a hissing-sound up the line of the cars, as air left the system and pistons pushed pads back to the wheels.

Buffkin's observation of the pads on the last car verified that the brakes were working from the first to the last car.

The conductor relayed his opinion to his engineer, "Brake test OK, you can take 'em off [release the brakes] when you are ready to go."

5:20 p.m.

The CSX voice recorder at the Jacksonville Command Center periodically inserts the time of day into all of its recorded dispatcher conversations.

"At the sound of the tone, the CSXT eastern standard time will be 17:10:15" (5:20 and 15 seconds p.m.).

The radio traffic between the CSX AU-Dispatcher, Crawford Boggs, and his Washington-Baltimore area railroad crews and local supervisors was lively. The "road-masters" are the company men responsible for keeping the tracks clear and functional in their territories.

AU Dispatcher: "Hello, [this is] Jacksonville."

Road-Master [for the subdivision between Baltimore and Washington]: "Yeah, hey dispatcher, Road-Master Gary Gammit, how you doin' there buddy?"

"Ain't worth a shit Gary, how 'bout yourself?"

"By god, I'm telling you; I'm asshole deep in snow myself."

"I heard that."

"Hah, hah. I'm checking in with you. Are you having any problems I should be aware of?"

AU: "I don't have the switches [at Savage and QN]. Neither crossover is working at Savage."

Gammit: "Well, the boys are up there right now."

"I was gonna say, are they're headed that way?"

"Well, I just talked to Kenny King and Lou Feld. They're up there right now.

AU: I wish you'd call my boss and tell him that. He's raising hell with me."

"Is that right?"

"Damn, he just [told] me I ain't [working hard enough]. I said, shit we're doing all we can do, Bud."

"I'll call Mark and get him straight."

"Alright, thank you."

The switch at QN was still inoperable and preventing Boggs from routing passenger trains leaving Washington onto the #1 main line track heading west toward Brunswick - the normal outbound only track. His plan "B" was firm. He would send them out on Track #2 - the inbound track coming from Brunswick and cross them back over to #1 eight miles west at Georgetown Junction.

At the same time, he decided to allow the Rock Runner freight waiting at QN on Track #1 to advance further up the parallel line past the Silver Spring station. There Boggs would hold it outside of the entrance to the Georgetown Junction interlocking until *The Capitol Limited* and the crunch of Brunswick MARC commuter trains could be moved out of Washington and through the Georgetown switches ahead of the empty freight.

The internal traffic manager for the Washington Terminal Yard was a local dispatcher, or "operator," who sat in the very old, two-story brick structure called "K" Tower. It may have been a tower in 1907 when it was built as the primary center for switching all the tracks in the yard, but ninety years later it looked like a dirty little lookout post at the end of the passenger platforms.

Throughout the years, however, the K-Tower operator has remained the supreme traffic-boss of the yard. In the days before remotely controlled switches, there were wooden handles inside the building that he would jerk back and forth to move the switches on the ground. Today his primary job is to instruct each train when it can enter or leave the vast expanse of tracks between him and the main line.

The AU dispatcher in Jacksonville, on the other hand, was empowered with the authority to decide the order or sequence in which each train leaves the station. Once they were out of the yard and onto the main, the train crews recognized the Jacksonville dispatcher as the commander of the road.

At 5:21 p.m. the CSX voice recorder in Jacksonville picked up the following conversation.

K Tower to Boggs: "[Amtrak 29] is ready for you."

AU Dispatcher: "Okay [tower]. Let me see, it's supposed to be 281's time [P281 is the MARC Brunswick commuter train scheduled to leave at 5:30]. He [29] is gonna be just ahead of P281."

K Tower: "P029 come down?"

Boggs to K-Tower: "Okay, let him come on, and then I'll look for P281 westbound behind [Amtrak] 29."

Since *The Capitol* was ready to depart close to the time that one of the MARC commuter trains was scheduled to leave, the AU dispatcher quickly decided to send the Amtrak out first. His rationale was simple; it was an express while the MARC commuter would be making numerous stops all the way up the line to Brunswick, including the Silver Spring station. Get the hare out ahead of the tortoise.

If the P281 had gone first, however, *The Capitol Limited* would have been delayed reaching the Georgetown Junction crossover, and this day would have passed into history as nothing more than a slightly dysfunctional, but otherwise normal, winter afternoon.

When any MARC or Amtrak train's departure time is near, the head-end conductor will push a button on a box attached to a post on the platform. That illuminates a small white light. A corresponding light inside the K-Tower informs the operator that he has a train ready to pull out within the next two to three minutes. If all the terminal yard switches are aligned, the operator will then switch on a second white light that gives the conductor on the platform the authority to notify his engineer that they can start whenever they are ready.

At 5:24, the second light on the platform box popped on. Conductor Buffkin remained on the platform at the back of the last car to make sure that some harried passenger, running late and sprinting down the platform, did not try to jump on the train once it had started to move. At 5:25 he gave Noble the all-clear, stepped inside and closed the rear door. *The Capitol* was finally on its way, one hour and twenty minutes behind schedule.

As soon as he ended his conversation with the tower operator, Dispatcher Boggs' attention wasdiverted to an incoming call on his outside (800) telephone line. The text of the conversation was automatically recorded on the voice monitor in Jacksonville.. This toll-free line was set up by CSX for use by their train crews in the event that normal radio communication between them and the dispatcher was interrupted, and they had to resort to finding a land-line telephone or one of the recently introduced, but not widely owned cell phones, to call Jacksonville.

AU Dispatcher: "CSX AU Jacksonville, over."

Female voice: "I just wanted to say I love you."

"I love you too, baby."

"I probably won't get to talk to you 'till Tuesday 'cause I'll be stuck in this house."

"Oh, that's alright 'cause I won't be around after today."

"You won't?"

AU: "No, I'll be racing this weekend."

Female voice: "You got off tomorrow?"

"Yeah.

"Well, I hope. Where's everyone coming from?"

"Kevin and his family, they're already here."

"Oh, they are?"

AU: "[They] came from Jacksonville, North Carolina."

Female voice: "I know that; where are the others?"

"Everybody else is here."

"Kenny is here."

"He's the one that's still there working, right?"

"Right."

"But, I thought you said the other one was coming?"

"Yeah, he did but he's the one from North Carolina."

"Oh, so he's already there? They're already at your house?"

"Yeah."

"Oh. How long have they been there?"

"They just got here."

"Okay."

AU: "Alright, I'll wave to ya."

Female voice: "Alright, baby."

"Wrap up good so you don't get a headache."

"I will."

"I love you and I'll talk to you on Tuesday."

"Okay baby."

"Bye-bye."

Then Boggs' normal railroad radio-traffic resumed:

"This is 252." (The MARC Camden-line commuter train
scheduled to leave Union Station at 5:12 p.m.)

"I told K Tower to tell you to change the engineer
and conductor on those orders. Did they call you already?"

AU Dispatcher: "Yes he did, over."

Train #252: "Okay, long as they did. We're running short
on time. [You think it will be] about 20 minutes for
my train to leave?"

[...] "I can barely hear you, sorry [...] Okay, I understand.
Thank you, Bill, AU Jacksonville is out."

Seventeen

In the months following the drama about to unfold, the second most controversial topic related to the accident would be train brakes.

Steel wheels on steel tracks significantly increase a train's load-carrying capacity and keep its consumption of fuel at a minimum. The ultimate game for mechanical train engineers has always been to find a way to transport goods and passengers across land with the efficiency of boats gliding through water. The railroads worked for over a 170 years to reduce wheel-to-rail friction by shrinking the contact areas on their locomotive and car wheels. Today, the newer rolling stock has reduced that space to about the width of a human finger. In its advertisements, CSX boasts that it can move a ton of cargo over 400 miles on one gallon of fuel.

At the same time, this quest for nominal-friction has substantially reduced a train's ability to stop. Automobiles and trucks have wide tire-to-road contact areas, and under dry conditions, the friction coefficient between their rubber surfaces and the asphalt beneath them (the resistance that the engine must overcome to roll their wheels) is nearly 75%. While that works against them when they are trying to gain speed, it helps when they are trying to slow down.

The coefficient between steel wheels and steel rails, however, is around 25%. That is very close to the value of rubber on ice. So, it is not improper to view trains running on a surface equivalent to ice on a normal asphalt highway. In addition, deceleration is directly related to not only speed, but weight.

A short, eighteen-car freight traveling at only 29 miles per hour (Lance Armstrong could probably cycle faster than that on a level surface without a sweat) will require the length of two football fields plus thirty additional yards to stop under full emergency braking. That distance increases by an amazing 4X when the speed is doubled to 60 miles per hour.

Up into the mid-1890s, several brakemen riding in both the engine and caboose remained prepared to spring into action when their engineer needed to slow down or stop the train. One of many specific whistle signals sent them climbing up onto the tops of the cars where they struggled to maintain their balance and turn brake wheels. After he had set one, the brakeman would jump the gap between the cars and tie down another. At the same time each man had to make sure that he didn't lock one of his brakes and cause the wheels to slide. That would grind a flat spot on their perimeters and prompt a swift notification from the railroad that it would be deducting the cost of fixing or replacing the wheels from the unfortunate employee's future paychecks.

If a brakeman happened to fall off a moving car and die, the railroad managers were only required to deliver his body to his family. The next morning they could hire another man for the same job at the rate of a dollar a day. Those who were severely injured simply lost their jobs. The companies were free from any form of liability. They openly claimed that they set good work standards, and that individual railroaders were responsible for their own survival, injuries or death. The states and federal government at the time supported that premise.

This early method of hand braking was not only extremely dangerous but also limited the length of trains to five or six cars and their speed to no more than 30 miles per hour.

In 1869, twenty-two-year-old George Westinghouse, a Civil War Union cavalry and naval veteran who loved to tinker with inventive ideas but had no training in railroad technology, submitted a patent application for an air-brake apparatus that could be applied by the engineer from inside his cab without using any onboard brakemen. Five years later, he refined his design into a system that has basically remained unchanged to this day.

Even though Westinghouse found a manufacturer for his product and widely advertised that it would permit railroad companies to run longer trains at faster speeds with fewer men and save thousands of lives, he was disappointed when none of the freight lines and only a few of the smaller passenger railroads sought to purchase it. Cheap labor coupled with no legal exposure for injuries or deaths was still the preferred method to operate.

At the same time, an unknown Iowa farmer entered the picture. Lorenzo Coffin, like George Westinghouse, had served in the Civil War (as a chaplain with the 32nd Iowa Regiment). Originally from New Hampshire, this Oberlin College graduate drifted west, bought several hundred acres of cheap land in Iowa and tried his hand at farming. To supplement his meager income, he took a job as a railroad land agent purchasing rights-of-way. One day in 1874, he happened to witness a brakeman lose several of his fingers working to join two freight cars using the crude, but standard, link-and-pin coupling device.

Appalled by the accident, Coffin began researching railroad statistics and discovered that between twenty-five- and thirty-thousand brakemen were maimed or killed each year in braking or coupling accidents. At the same time he read about an inventor named Eli Janney (a former Confederate officer from Loudoun County, Virginia) who had recently patented an automatic coupling device that would not require men to stand between the cars. After the war, Janney had worked as a clerk in a dry goods store in Alexandria, Virginia, and spent most of his lunch breaks whittling his concept of a "knuckle coupler" out of a block of wood.

At age 51, preacher Coffin embraced the Westinghouse and Janney inventions and began a one-man crusade to get the railroads to use them by arousing elected officials and the general public. Over the next nine years he toured the State of Iowa recounting death and dismemberment horror stories as well as writing hundreds of letters to public officials. In 1883 he managed to get himself appointed Iowa's first railroad commissioner and used that office to draft a railroad safety-appliance act. Even though the state legislature enacted it into law, they looked the other way when the powerful railroads chose to ignore its provisions.

Then Coffin decided to take his campaign nationwide, and the railroad companies immediately launched a counter offensive to publicly characterize him as "the "little beaded air-brake fanatic." Years later, in March of 1893, however, Coffin and his band of disciples finally gained enough political support to push a bill through the U.S. Congress that required all American railroads to install air brakes and automatic couplers on their trains. President Benjamin Harrison, a conservative who was known to favor big business over labor, signed it into law on his last day in office and gave the pen to seventy-year-old Coffin. Most of the railroads took the full five-year implementation period to comply with its provisions, but the casualties among trainmen eventually fell by 60 percent.

Today, every train has two primary braking systems, automatic air brakes and dynamic braking. The first one operates throughout the entire train and the second one only on the locomotive.

Automatic air brakes provide 90% of a train's braking-capacity. They are called service brakes, pneumatic brakes and friction brakes. Briefly, this is how they work:

A compressor on the locomotive compacts air and routes it back through the entire length of the train inside a continuous metal tube called a train-line or brake-pipe. The air flow bridges the spaces between the cars inside flexible hoses called "glad hands." Along its journey, the compressed air fills two types of storage tanks, or "reservoirs," located beneath the floor of each car. The service reservoir holds a supply for use in normal, everyday braking, and the emergency reservoir remains primed and available as an additional source of braking power if it is needed.

The brilliance of Westinghouse's design was that it was based on a fail-safe operational concept that ran counter to normal logic. It used the *absence* of air pressure in the line to *open* the reservoirs and apply the brakes, and the *presence* of air pressure in the line to *release* the brakes. That was considered fail-safe because a sudden loss of pressure from a broken or disconnected line would automatically stop the train.

Down near each set of wheels, the reservoirs connect with brake cylinders. The cylinders contain rods that can push brake pads against the surface of the wheels to slow and stop them. When the reservoirs release their compressed air, it pushes the rods and pads toward the wheels. When air leaves the system, the rods and pads withdraw from the wheels.

What made this concept workable was a simple, two-way control valve that Westinghouse placed at the entrance to each reservoir. Only the amount of air pressure present in the brake line moved those valves. When the engineer activated his service brakes, air left the train line, pressure dropped, and the control valves moved in one direction to *open* their service reservoirs and release stored air into the cylinders (brake pads against wheels).

Conversely, when the engineer "released" the brakes, the outside holes in the train line opened, pressure dropped and the little valves moved in the opposite direction. That released the air holding the pads against the wheels. At the same time a new supply of air from the locomotive replenished the supply in each of the cars' reservoirs.

Air brake applications and releases are instantaneous, not gradual. All of the brake shoes either firmly press against, or retreat from, all the wheels in tandem. When an engineer wants to apply a small amount of braking, he makes a "partial reduction" by moving his air-brake handle slightly to the right. The amount of air pressure that leaves his train line shows up on his gauge as ten pounds, twenty pounds, etc. and the brakes partially apply at those rates.

Every veteran commuter has experienced a day when his train suddenly rolled to a stop in the middle of nowhere. The conductors climbed out and walked the length of the cars. What happened? The answer is usually, "We lost our air." A foreign object on the track (such as tree limb or even a deer walking across the tracks) has bounced up and disconnected one of the air hoses that hang down between the cars. The system's air leaked out, the pressure dropped, and the brakes automatically applied.

The engine brake, also known as the independent brake, is part of this same system but gets its air through a separate line from the engine and only works to slow and stop the locomotive itself. The engineer uses this brake when switching freight around a rail yard and the cars he is pulling or pushing are disconnected from the flow of air in the continuous train line. On other occasions, he may apply his engine brake to gently slow and "bunch up" a long freight moving down a hill.

The second major system is called "dynamic braking." By first shifting his throttle into idle and then moving another lever on his panel, the engineer can gradually or quickly disconnect the electric power traveling from his alternator to the traction motors down on his locomotive's axles. Contrary to popular belief, the motors do not move into reverse, but simply shut down in increments based on how far the engineer moves the handle through (5) different positions, like turning a rheostat knob for a light. As the current disappears, the power-starved armatures on the traction motors no longer drive the wheels but begin to resist their continued rotation and retard the progress of the train.

The braking sensation is very similar to the one an automobile driver feels when downshifting an automatic or standard transmission. Each shift further downward slows the car a little more. Engineers often use this system to slow the decent of a long freight train moving down a steep grade. A prolonged application of the regular air-brakes can grind down and eventually destroy their brake pads. Traction motors are more resilient. The dynamic brake by itself, however, is not designed to quickly slow, or fully stop, a train.

When an engineer moves his air brake handle all the way over to its "emergency" position, that action is called "going to the big hole" or "dumping your air." At that instant, several things happen at the same time. The air in the long brake pipe instantaneously vents to the outside, and the compressed in both the service reservoirs and *emergency reservoirs* pop out like corks leaving bottles of champagne.

"Clean your clock" is another old railroad expression that describes what the engineer's air-brake gauge looks like when the emergency brakes are applied. As the air rushes out of the train-line, the hand on the face of the clocklike, gauge drops to zero.

In emergency braking, two additional things happen; the engineer's throttle automatically flips into the idle position and the traction motors totally lose their source of electric current. This dynamic braking feature is somewhat slow to engage, however, usually taking a full 10 seconds. Dynamic braking helps to guarantee that the wheels will not lock and slide, unless, unless the "reverser" (the lever that controls the direction of travel) is moved. If the engineer moves that, the dynamic process will cancel, leaving the train with only its air brakes to manage a deceleration. Although this is normally insignificant in routine train movement, it would prove to be a critical element later in this winter day.

Eighteen

5:27 p.m.

The Capitol Limited lumbers through a vast spider-web of interconnected switches and tracks as it leaves the Washington Terminal Yard. The huge locomotives shake the ground beneath them. When he reaches the junction with the main line at the QN interlocking (milepost 2.1), Engineer Don Noble realizes that the Jacksonville dispatcher has routed him out on Track #2 for the first few miles of his trip northwest.

Dispatcher Boggs is not required to tell Noble or the conductors why he has shifted them onto to the normal inbound rails. He also is not obligated to alert the crews on trains coming from he other direction on the same set of tracks that they may be required to stop soon. On the other hand, forwarding such information is not prohibited. Based on their individual operating styles, many dispatchers choose to inform crews about upcoming anomalies. The railroad has always touted its time-proven rule of the road; just obey the signals and everything will work out fine.

Noble advances his throttle over to the sixth notch, and his engines groan in response. With its fifteen-car payload and 330-foot rise in grade from Union Station to milepost 6.3 at Takoma Park, Maryland, *The Capitol,* even with two powerful engines pulling it, will strain to make 54 miles per hour.

Inside the cab of the older, F-40 locomotive, Noble and his assistant engineer ignore the heavy and constant vibration. Neither one could hold a Styrofoam cup of coffee without spilling it all over themselves. From the outside, however, his engines look like ships gently rolling through swells in a moderate sea.

Simple wipers move the light falling snow back and forth and off the front windows. The steady roar of the diesel motor and alternator drown out normal conversation. "Yell" is the normal volume inside the cab. An open speaker on the control stand blares crackling static and unintelligible chatter from the radio transmissions of nearby trains. No one but a seasoned railroader could distinguish what people are saying.

The only way Don Noble can recognize an incoming message directed to him is to catch the call number of his train (P029) at its inception. If he wants to "call a signal" or speak with his conductors in the cars behind him, he can either push a button and talk into a microphone on the panel in front of him or lift and use a conventional-style telephone handset located on the left wall of his control stand. Engineers usually prefer the latter to more clearly transmit or receive messages because of the surrounding engine noises.

Every 45 to 90 seconds (shorter intervals at higher speeds and longer intervals at slower speeds) an annoying buzzer or siren will sound if Noble has not moved the brake, throttle or whistle-handles during that period. That is the "alerter," a safety device installed to monitor the engineer's general consciousness and reflexes. When it starts screaming, he must punch a disk-like, "touch-off" button with the side of his fist, flip a switch or move one of his normal controls to shut it off. Otherwise the train will begin to stop. In the old, old days, an engineer had to physically depress what was called a "dead-man's" pedal to the floor with his foot during the entire trip to prove that he was in his seat and alert.

Noble admits that the interior cab of the newer Amtrak locomotives, like the model GE P40 that is in back of him, are far more comfortable and less noisy, but he likes the "ancient" model he is operating up front today.

"I really prefer the F-40," he said, "it is like driving your 14-year-old car. You're used to it. You know what it can do in most circumstances. The newer engines don't accelerate like this one. In fact, they take some time to catch up to the F40 and can't slow down as fast. If you've got two F40's, you've really got some power."

Today, he has only one.

As Noble's Amtrak enters the main line on its way to Silver Spring, Jacksonville Dispatcher Boggs answers another call on his outside 800 line.

"CSX AU Jacksonville."

Female voice: "Hey Mr. Love."

AU Dispatcher: "Hey"

"What are you doing?"

AU: "I am 'bout to work my fanny off."

"Poor baby."

AU: "I'll be skin and bones [by the] time I get out."

"Oh, Lord. Maybe I better come in and take over for you."

"I tell ya. What can I do for you?"

"I just called Kenny. [Jordan] answered the phone and she asked where I was. I told her I was home. She said, 'Thought you were coming back to work.' I said, 'Yeah, but Crawford had to take my car, I wanted to bring it home first.' She said, 'Well what time you coming over?' I said, Oh what time you having dinner?' [...] [She said] 'Kenny and I are going out to dinner.'"

"Do what?"

"Yeah!" [...] So then I [thought]....well maybe they want me to come over to baby-sit. I said, 'Is Kevin and [everybody going]?'

She said, 'Ken and I cause Kevin doesn't feel too good. Just Kenny and I are going out.'"

"You know what you should have done, just asked him if they wanted to come over to the house. You'll fix something there. [...] Kenny's taking her out for her Valentine's Day."

"So then I talked to Kenny. I said, 'Is Kevin and [?] going?'

He said, 'No Jordan wants me to take her out for Valentine.'

You know, how rude."

"With them, [what can you say?]"

"Right, Kenny said, 'Well you come over here and visit with Kevin and the kids.'"

"They'll be over our house tomorrow."

"Yeah"

"I don't know."

"[What's with them] carrying Chris out to dinner or something because, I mean, she said that she was gonna cook dinner tonight.

Everybody come over and I'll cook dinner."

AU: "She did. She fixed food."

"[Food] for everybody to eat while they go out and have sex.

"Yeah, oh well."

"I couldn't believe it when she said that. I was shocked."

"I bet you were. Hang in there."

"Alright babe."

"You rushing me off?'

"Yeah, I gotta go. I'm covered up."

"Y'all covered up?"

"Yeah."

"I got company or [a call coming in]."

"Better be a male."

"Yeah, it is."

CSX time-and-voice recorder:

"At the sound of the tone, CSXT Eastern Standard Time will be 17:30:08" (5:30 and 8 seconds).

Engineer Jobe Breeden has his MARC P279 one mile west of Silver Spring, fifteen minutes ahead of Don Noble, and beginning to pass through the Georgetown Junction from Track #2 over to Track #1. The signal there is a "medium clear" which translates into two directives – the engineer must maintain a speed of less than 30 m.p.h. through the switches, and once he is on Track #1, he can move up to the normal limit of 70.

Passenger Geraldine Dykes feels the car sway from side to side as it negotiates the crossover. She glances up from her paperback book and suddenly realizes that the scenery outside looks totally unfamiliar. Picking up her purse and backpack, she makes her way through the cars in search of a conductor. She finds Leechel Reynolds.

He immediately activates his two-way radio to contact Engineer Breeden. "P279, have you made contact with P286 coming down from Brunswick?"

"No, not yet," Breeden says, "and he is not in sight."

Reynolds continues, "See if you can get in touch with him when you can. We have a lady passenger that got on the wrong train. She was supposed to go to Laurel. If P286 has not passed Kensington by the time we get there, we will leave her off at the platform. Tell him to pick her up and take her back to Union Station."

Breeden makes his scheduled stop at the Kensington station and notifies his conductor that the P286 has still not come into view. Reynolds tells Dykes that she should get off there. An in-bound train will be coming the other way in a few minutes. Dykes gingerly steps down from the coach into six inches of snow, waits for the MARC to pull out and crosses the tracks a group of local homeward-bound commuters. She removes an umbrella from her backpack, opens it and begins her vigil on the south-side platform.

Standing nearby in his civilian clothes, is twenty-three-year-old Mike Charissis, Navy ensign and third-year medical student at the Uniformed Services Medical School on the campus of the Naval Hospital in nearby Bethesda, Maryland. He had decided earlier that afternoon to try to catch the train into Washington to meet some friends for dinner. This is only his second trip into D.C. by train.

Inside the Jacksonville, Florida, CSX bunker, Dispatcher Boggs is consumed with Northern weather complications. The Baltimore-Camden line is backed up with freights heading toward Washington and MARC commuter trains trying to get out of that city.

Ricky Orr makes an unscheduled stop at the Rockville station to drop off Tim Fowler, one of the Job Corps students. The delay takes less than one minute. He then accelerates up to 74 m.p.h. over the next three minutes, and starts to gently back down his speed as he approaches the Garrett Park station. This is one of the potential "flag" stops where MARC crews are required to pick up anyone waiting on the platform. Today, all he can see are several kids throwing snowballs at him. Orr continues running at 53 m.p.h. over the remaining one and one-half miles to Kensington.

If nothing else changes, the P286 will enter Georgetown Junction at 5:38 p.m.

Nineteen

5:33 p.m.

Jobe Breeden's MARC P279 is barely up to speed moving westward from Kensington toward Rockville when he finally catches sight of Ricky Orr's train coming across the Rock Creek Bridge ahead. Before Breeden can speak, Orr comes on the radio line with a warning. "You got kids up ahead of ya along the track."

Breeden's train, however, has just started passing over an audible defect-detector embedded in the tracks, and its preemptory broadcast on the crews' radios interferes with their conversation. Breeden asks Engineer Orr to repeat his message. Orr says, "Be on the lookout for some kids that are down by the Garrett Park platform throwing snowballs."

Breeden replies, "Thanks. Everything is okay behind *me*."

Their comments are part of a normal check procedure required of engineers on commuter trains that are approaching each other on parallel tracks.. They each conduct a visual inspection of the other man's unit as it passes and also report any potentially dangerous situations that they have noticed coming up or down the line - people walking on the tracks, debris placed on the rails or kids throwing objects at passing trains.

Breeden quickly informs Orr that he dropped-off a female passenger with a green backpack at Kensington for him to pick up. Orr acknowledges the request, and then *his* train rolls over the same detector. Neither engineer can hear anything more except the canned recording. The two MARCs flash past each other. Breeden did not think to mention that he came out of D.C. on Track #2 and crossed to #1 a few miles back.

Seconds later Orr's eastbound commuter train passes the wayside block-signal located almost 300 yards ahead of the Kensington station. It is supposed to be displaying two yellow lights arranged in a diagonal pattern. That translates into an approach signal, or a slow-down indication and means that Ricky must immediately reduce his speed to 30 miles per hour, continue at that rate through the entire block and remain prepared to stop at the next signal two miles ahead at Georgetown Junction.

Orr immediately begins braking for the unscheduled stop to pick up the lady that got on the wrong train. Kensington Station is hidden around a slight curve to the right. He and Jim Quillen strain to look through the blowing snow to see if their passenger is there. Jimmy Major begins walking back through the front car past the Job Corps students to open its rear door.

The location of the wayside signal that Orr just passed, #100, is relatively new. Ever since they took over the line, CSX knew that it had a problem with the length of some of the blocks, especially the distance between Kensington and Georgetown Junction. It measured almost 9,000 feet (1.70 miles) and their standard braking allowance for long freight trains in a subdivision that included passenger trains traveling over 60 miles per hour was 13,000 feet, or 2.46 miles.

In 1985, MARC formally requested CSXT to cooperate with them in implementing their plan to add 22 more commuter trains on the Camden and Brunswick lines. CSXT countered with the claim that it was limited in its ability to accommodate that much additional traffic without lengthening some of the blocks. They clearly saw it as an opportunity to secure public funds to pay for improvements that would also allow them to run longer freights over two-thirds of the Baltimore Division.

The parties reached an accommodation. Over the next six years they would create a few new interlockings and expand some of the blocks. That, however, would require moving some signals. Construction began in 1991 with the Federal Railroad Administration (FRA) contributing 75% of the $13 million cost. The State of Maryland and CSXT agreed to split the remainder.

One of the "improvements" was the relocation of signal #100 from its location almost a mile east of Kensington (toward Washington) to a point 300 yards west of the Kensington station. That significantly improved the length of the block between there and Georgetown Junction.

In its new spot, however, the signal created a subtle, but potentially dangerous problem for engineers running east-bound passenger trains. With the occasional task of stopping at the Kensington station, they could possibly forget the aspect of the new signal behind them. Technical studies called "human-factor analyses" are usually required in federally funded, railroad-modification projects in order to detect and correct such design flaws. For some unknown reason, none of the three participating parties; the federal government, the State of Maryland or CSX thought it was necessary to perform this simple study for the Kensington signal transplant. That decision, or lack of a decision, would help to create the upcoming disaster.

At the other end of this block, the Georgetown Junction interlocking with its double set of crossover rails is set behind a long and blind, right-to-left curve. An engineer approaching from Kensington cannot see the interlocking signals until he is almost upon them. And just beyond the wayside towers, there are not that many yards to the crossover switches. No room to accommodate an error.

Ricky Orr aligns the rear of his lead passenger coach to the Kensington platform and his MARC train slows to a stop. Jimmy Major opens the rear door of the cab car and remains inside. Geraldine Dykes steps into the vestibule, recognizes her conductor friend from his days on the Camden line and smiles. She has always liked to call him Jolly Jim and remembers pointing to his name on his uniform coat and saying, "You're too short to be a Major." Over the years she has had numerous brief conversations with him about finding her a quiet spot to sit where she could read her book. Today he directs her and Mike Charissis to the second car with the comment, "It has been a little noisy up front."

Mike Charissis walks down the aisle to the sixth row of seats on his right. Dykes sits in the first row on the same side, changes her mind and moves across the aisle. She pulls her MARC train schedule out of her backpack and notes that the arrival time for the P286 at Union Station is 5:50. *With a little luck,* she thinks, *I can still catch the 6:05 Camden-line train home to Laurel.*

The stop at Kensington has taken slightly more than sixty seconds. There is still about a half an hour of fading daylight remaining, but the snow-laden cloud cover makes the landscape look darker than normal. The normal scheduled travel time between Kensington (at milepost 11.0) and Georgetown Junction (8.3) is 3 minutes and 45 seconds. Even though the maximum authorized passenger-train speed in that recently expanded block is 70 m.p.h., the *Approach* signal at Kensington (now behind the MARC crew) has temporarily reduced it to 30.

Jimmy Major walks back to the cab compartment and leaves the interior door open behind him. Ricky Orr eases the train away from the platform and quickly accelerates up to 58 miles per hour. It doesn't take long for a light, three-coach passenger train to move from zero to sixty.

Has Orr forgotten the last signal, the yellow one before the Kensington station? Perhaps he is he ignoring the temporarily mandated 30 m.p.h. speed limit with the thought that he can easily slow down right before Georgetown Junction? Is it possible that that the Kensington lights were green? A minute later Engineer Orr backs his speed downward, apparently observing the long-standing limitation of 55 m.p.h. (when traveling under a clear signal) between Milepost 10.6 and Milepost 9.5 at the gentle "S" curves near Forest Glen.

Quillen and Major both continue to linger in the cab compartment with Engineer Orr. The bridge passing over the Washington Beltway is coming up just ahead and the exotic-looking white Mormon Temple with its gold spires will soon be visible off to the right through the bare winter trees. Orr moves his throttle into the 8th (highest) notch as his train comfortably moves from 55 to 63 mph. It's Friday, the day before a three-day, holiday weekend; the weather does not look good, and it will be nice to get home.

Damien Benetiz, one of the Job Corps students, feels a sudden urge to stand up. He looks up the aisle through the open cab door at the back of one of the conductors while he continues to talk to the friend behind him. Kevin Williams calls to Rodney Crawford to come forward so they too can talk. Crawford starts walking up the aisle.

With the delay, and Engineer Orr's increased speed, the MARC P286's probable arrival time at Georgetown Junction has now advanced to 5:38:40.

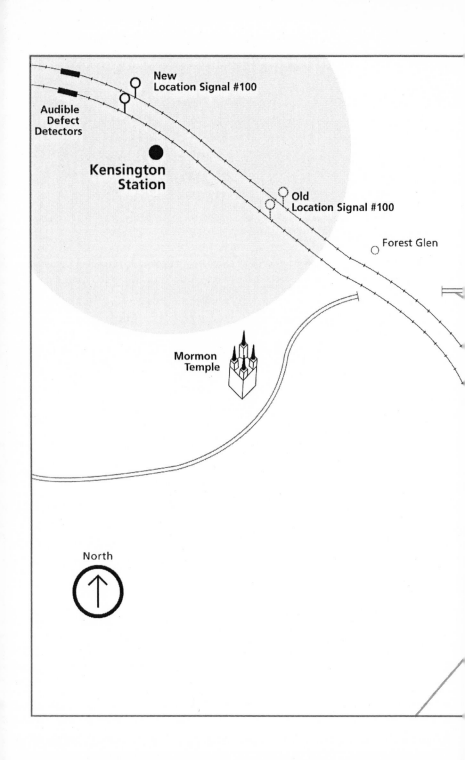

Audible
Defect
Detectors

New
Location Signal #100

Kensington
Station

Old
Location Signal #100

Forest Glen

Mormon
Temple

North

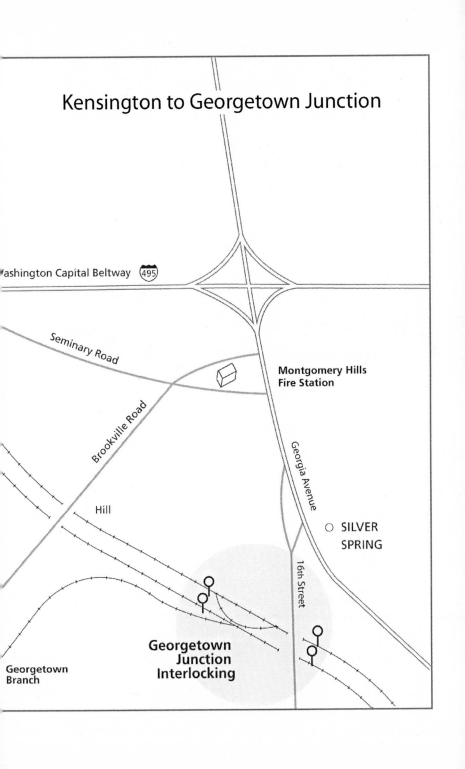

Kensington to Georgetown Junction

Washington Capital Beltway 495

Seminary Road

Brookville Road

Montgomery Hills
Fire Station

Georgia Avenue

Hill

○ SILVER
SPRING

16th Street

Georgetown
Junction
Interlocking

Georgetown
Branch

Twenty

Life is like a mountain railway, with an engineer who's brave;
We must make the run successful, from the cradle to the grave;
Always mindful of distractions, do you duty, never fail;
Keep your hand upon the throttle, and your eye upon the rail.
As you roll across the trestle, spanning Jordan's swelling tide;
You'll behold the Union Depot, into which your train will glide:
There you'll meet the Superintendent,
God the Father, God the Son;
With the hearty, joyous plaudit,
Weary pilgrim, welcome home!

> --- Portion of the hymn, "Life's Railway to Heaven."
> Eliza R. Snow, M.E. Abbey and Charles D. Tillman. 1890

5:36 p.m.

The Capitol Limited has completed its gradual uphill climb from Washington and is approaching the Silver Spring station. It is no longer a scheduled stop for Amtrak. From that point the grade begins to drop slightly. Don Noble is still operating his train under the approach-medium signal that he passed at Takoma Park, and is holding its speed to 30 m.p.h. That signal meant that he will not be asked to stop at the entrance to the next block (Georgetown Junction), and the switches there have been set for him to move over to Track #1.

Engineer M.R. Barnhouse and Conductor Scott Hodges are the only crew members onboard the empty Rock Runner freight that Dispatcher Boggs has been holding at the entrance to Georgetown Junction on Track #1. Both are in their mid-twenties and sitting in their idling locomotive waiting for the Amtrak to come past them on the left. When that happens, the Jacksonville dispatcher may release them to move up the road behind it. Their return trip from the Washington area to West Virginia is already four hours behind schedule. Hodges, who is working off the extra board today, rambles on about what he is going to do when he gets home.

5:37:15 p.m.

Noble rolls his *Capitol* by the Silver Spring station. He and Assistant Engineer Fratangelo can now see the rear of the Rock Runner holding on Track #1 off to their right across the Metro subway tracks. Noble turns to Joey and says, "Ah, *that's* why we've been reversing" (running on the inbound track to move around a slow freight).

Within seconds, his two locomotives come alongside the freight and start into the sharp curve preceding Georgetown Junction. Their speed has dropped down to 27 miles per hour. A medium-clear signal on the wayside tower ahead (two vertical green lights over a white one on the post) flashes into view just before the 16th Street overpass. Noble moves his throttle over from notch 3 to notch 4 as his train passes the lights on the circular mast to his right. The bridge overhead frames the scene before him, a half-a-mile section of straight track with the Georgetown Junction crossover less than 300 feet ahead.

At that instant, Ricky Orr's MARC P286 glides out of the long curve that precedes the other end of Noble's visual straightaway. His three cars, and pushing locomotive, are up to 65 miles per hour and covering 95.4 feet per second as they pass under the Brookville Road Bridge. A high bank on the left obscures any view of the upcoming Georgetown Junction interlocking.

Not until they reach the end of the curve, a point 1,527 feet before the crossover, will Orr or the two conductors with him in the cab be able to see the wayside signals. They are not anticipating anything unusual.

And then, *WHACK*! An unbelievable sight smacks them in the face - small lights off in the distance - red lights, stop signals on the trackside towers, and beyond that, the headlamp of a locomotive moving out of a curve.

Orr, Major and Quillen try to rationalize the scene in front of them. Is the locomotive on their track or the adjacent one? Is it slowing down? No one will ever know what was said.

One second passes. Orr's right hand wraps around the throttle handle and his left hand grabs the brake. Every muscle in his body is poised for action. He notches the throttle back from the #8 to the #4 position. Another second passes.

Damian Benetiz is standing in the aisle of the MARC cab car looking through the open door into the engineer's compartment. He watches as one of the conductors jerks forward, appears to look intently at something out the front window, then rocks back and leans forward again. A third second leaps into history.

5:38:28 p.m.

Engineer Orr's left wrist snaps the brake handle into the emergency position. All the air-brake reservoirs on his cars and engine release their pent-up, stored power. Thirty-two cylinder pistons thrust their brake pads against thirty-two wheels. Dynamic braking through the traction motors will automatically follow. His engine throttle flips into idle.

Orr's three seconds of hesitation, however, have consumed almost 300 additional feet of track.

The two conductors, concerned about their young student passengers, turn and bolt through the doorway into the passenger compartment. Jimmy Major is in the lead. The sudden deceleration of the train, however, has created a force that pulls them backward. They grab the seat backs hand over hand and slowly move themselves through the car. Both are screaming the same warning in a slightly different way; "Move to the back! Get down! Brace yourselves!"

Benetiz and his friend, Rodney Crawford, watch them come up the aisle and wonder why they are yelling. For a moment the two students freeze. Benetiz turns and scrambles toward the rear of the car. A few others follow him. Those who are just waking up from naps continue to sit in a semi-conscious haze.

The P286 has covered another 540 feet, and is down to 52 miles per hour. The dynamic braking has not had enough time to kick in.

Onboard the Amtrak engine, Don Noble watches the MARC's headlight rapidly sweep into the long straightaway before him. "Hey Joey," he calls to his assistant engineer, "Look at *this* son-of-a-bitch! Look at this bastard! We have the lights, and he's not going to stop!"

A rush of adrenalin puts everything on the table. Braking is the obvious first option. Noble grabs the air-brake handle. He knows that there is not enough time or track to avoid a collision, but he can see that he is a lot closer to the upcoming switch than the oncoming train. Remembering that the first seven cars behind his engines are filled with mail and baggage, not passengers, he makes a decision. *Maybe, just maybe,* he decides, *I have just enough time to gain a little speed and get my locomotives far enough into the crossover so that this guy will hit us at a glancing angle.*

His left hand comes off the brake handle as his right hand grabs the throttle and jerks it over into the 8th notch. *The Capitol Limited* is now only 250 feet from the switch and slowly gaining speed.

Joey Frantangelo eyes are locked the oncoming train's light. *"Oh my god,"* he thinks, *"it's a freight, and we're going to hit head on."* Rising from his seat, he silently moves around behind his engineer, opens the locomotive-compartment door and steps out onto the ice-covered metal ladder, fumbles his grip and catapults through the air at 30 miles per hour down into the snow, gravel and brush beside the tracks.

In the lead car of the MARC P286, some of the Job Corps kids have started to crouch down behind the seatbacks. Others, including Eric Garcia and Tyrai Boyer are almost at the back of the coach. Many have not reacted at all. Rodney Crawford continues to stand in place, staring at the bight light of the oncoming locomotive through the front window. Major and Quillen continue up the aisle, barking at the students to get down and brace themselves. They have struggled to make it a third of the way back through the car. The conductors move past the four in the forward section who are just waking including the two seventeen-year-old girls, Diana Hanvichid and Lakeisha Marshall, as well as Carlos Byrd.

The MARC train continues braking over another 460 feet of track, but it has ramped down to only to 46 miles per hour. Orr now knows that he will not be able to stop and can see that the oncoming engineer is not slowing. The house-sized Amtrak locomotive looms larger and larger in front of him. Its headlight is blinding.

The two trains are now only eight seconds apart.

5:38:32 p.m.

There is one last thing that Ricky Orr can try. His hand moves the "reverser" handle to change the direction of the locomotive that is pushing his train from the rear. It is already at idle, however, and cannot suddenly gear up to begin pulling against the fast forward motion of the train. That will take a minute, a minute Orr doesn't have. Most importantly, moving the reverser cancels the engine's dynamic-braking and its ability to prevent the wheels from sliding.

An impact is inevitable, but with the dynamic braking shut down, it will take the MARC *less* time, *six seconds* instead of *seven,* to cover the remaining 407 feet to the spot where *The Capitol Limited* is racing to cross over to the other set of tracks. If Orr had that one second, the lead Amtrak engine could advance an additional 46 feet into the crossover and his MARC cab car would strike only the left *side* of the *second* Amtrak locomotive. Shifting the reverser lever prevents that from happening.

The Capitol is notched-out" in its highest throttle position, but has only accelerated from 27 to 31 miles per hour over the last six seconds, the longest six seconds in Don Noble's life. His two Amtrak locomotives are now covering 45 feet per second in their race to the crossover tracks.

Time is almost up.

Noble's attention is completely focused on the switch. It seems to be rushing toward him in slow motion. The tracks ahead are white with accumulated snow, but the areas around the switch points are clear and visible due to the thirteen kerosene switch-heaters that are spouting continuous small flames onto the steel rails there. He can also see that the switch is set in his favor to cross over to Track #1.

He yells at his locomotive, begging the big F-40 to move faster. "Come on baby. Come on baby. Let's rock and roll!"

The crossover is only a few yards away and Noble is screaming, "We got it! We got it! It's ours!"

The two MARC conductors instinctively sense that they need to seek shelter, NOW.. Jim Quillen ducks between two sections of seats, and Jimmy Major falls onto the floor a few feet away. They are both halfway through the car.

5:38:40 p.m.

The MARC train's headlight illuminates Noble's entire windshield, but he is not looking at it. His eyes are frozen on the switch points on the tracks below him. He watches them disappear under him as his locomotive rushes into the crossover. Even though the parallel Tracks #1 and #2 are less than 10 feet apart, 270 feet of crossover rails were built at Georgetown Junction to gradually span that short distance at angle of about 15 degrees (from 12:00 to 12:03 on the face of a clock) to permit trains to cross over at higher speeds.

Ricky Orr knows there is nothing more he can do. His MARC commuter train is still in full emergency braking, but its speed has been dropping slowly. It now shows 39 miles per hour. He turns to his left and steps through the door behind him into the passenger compartment. The nose of *The Capitol's* lead engine is halfway across the stretch of rails leading over to Track#1. Another one half of a second and the front ends of both trains will clear each other.

The left front of the huge Amtrak locomotive and the left front of the diminutive MARC cab car meet at a combined speed of 70 miles per hour. A terrible howl of crushing metal reverberates off of buildings a mile away. The force of the impact hurls Don Noble's body from one side of his metal cab to the other and back. His foot smashes out one of his side windows.

With its high-riding, heavy ballast platform, the Amtrak slices into the cab car like a can opener. The only point of token resistance, a vertical collision post installed inside the left front of the MARC car to withstand 300,000 pounds of inward pressure, snaps at its base like a dry twig.

Tyrai Boyer, thinks a bolt of lightning has hit the top of the car. Inside, chunks of debris fly throughout the coach. The students are jerked backward, forward and sideways. Some flop out into the aisle and others have their heads smacked against the windows, walls and seatbacks.

Everything between the floor and the roof on the left side of the MARC cab car - for 36 feet back - is swept away in the blink of an eye. Sturdy sheet-metal exterior, windows, luggage racks and seats are scooped out of the coach and remain attached to the front of the Amtrak locomotive. The first five rows of MARC passenger seats on the left are gone. The next five are crushed flat. No one was sitting in them.

The remaining floor and undercarriage of the MARC cab car glide unobstructed beneath the Amtrak locomotive's elevated ballast platform and smash into that engine's lead pilot-truck (wheel assembly and traction motors). The truck, in turn, rockets backward into the front of the locomotive's low-hanging, 1,800-gallon fuel tank. Hundreds of gallons of diesel fuel spray out of the single-compartment tank across the space between the trains and into the huge ragged hole in the passing MARC coach. The students, conductors and engineer are thoroughly soaked.

The forward portion of the cab car bursts into a fireball as the lead truck of the Amtrak locomotive violently compresses the large nickel cadmium batteries on the lower side of the

MARC car. The resulting thermal-chemical explosion, though small, is enough to ignite the fine mist of airborne diesel fuel.

Engineer Orr is severely scorched by the blast and pulled, or tossed, out of the large opening by the violent sideways movement of the cars. His battered and burned body would later be found on the ground between the sets of tracks.

Both trains rappel off each other in different directions. The lead Amtrak engine jumps over the tracks to its right and dives into the loose gravel on the ground. Even with its front wheels missing, the F40 locomotive continues to be pushed from behind by the forward momentum of the second engine and 15 trailing cars (almost three million pounds of rolling energy). It is rotated clockwise and disconnected from the rest of the train. Engineer Noble is crumpled up on the floor of his cab, unable to do anything as his engine plows through snow, dirt and rock along the top edge of a steep cliff.

The MARC cab car's front truck assembly separates from its mooring as the damaged coach becomes airborne over another 40 feet. When it slams down on the dislodged wheels and axles, they spike the plywood and metal floor upward two feet in the exact area where Conductor Jimmy Major has taken refuge. A jagged piece of metal punctures his neck, severing a carotid artery. Considering what is about to happen, his lapse into unconsciousness is merciful. He quickly bleeds to death. As the MARC cab car hits the ground, it shoves an entire section of the old parallel and intersecting Georgetown branch line, rails and crossties, over to edge of the embankment. The train cars come to rest also leaning in that direction..

Noble's off-the-tracks lead locomotive finally disconnects from the second engine and lurches to an abrupt stop. Its nose bobs and teeters at the edge of the hill looking down into the woods toward the Park Sutton. The cars behind keep moving long enough to push the second Amtrak engine past Noble's. It too finally leaves the tracks and stops, wedged between the

MARC's trailing locomotive and the back of Noble's. None of *The Capitol Limited* coaches turn over, but two of the material-handling cars have left the tracks and buckled into a severe V-formation.

Parts of the MARC's large batteries remain jammed inside the Amtrak's smashed and detached fuel tank that is now down the tracks. The instant fireball quickly disappears, but the students and conductors in the middle of the coach remain covered in a film of cold, black, flammable liquid.

The second MARC coach, the one in which Dykes and Charissis are riding, is also leaning to the right, but at a more severe angle than the cab car. Both are being prevented from toppling over and tumbling down the hill by their tenuous couplings to cars forward and/or behind. The area around the second coach's left-front door is crushed inward.

Engineer Don Noble is still wired. He doesn't feel his bruises and broken ankle. Slowing pulling himself over to the opening where his side window used to be, he peers out into a dull white void and thinks that he has lost his eyesight. He closes his eyes, rubs them with his hand, opens them and realizes that he is just looking at dark snow on the ground.

Shaking his head, he says out loud, "Jesus Christ. A guy could get killed doing this shit."

Some of *The Capitol Limited* passengers have been severely knocked around, but none of them are seriously injured.

Michael French, the young Amtrak electrician who had been riding in the second locomotive to monitor its repaired electrical system, is unconscious.

On the idling Rock Runner freight, Randy Barnhouse and Scott Hodges initially ignored the Amtrak as it rolled past them. Engineer Barnhouse, however, happened to be looking out his windshield on the right side of the cab and caught a glimpse of the MARC P286 coming out of the distant curve.

Then it was blocked from his view by the Amtrak's lead locomotive moving into the crossover. A couple of seconds later everything in front of the two men started to disintegrate – an explosion and flames, the Amtrak engine lifting off the tracks and turning sideways, mail and baggage cars jackknifing.

Hodges climbs down out of his locomotive and starts jogging up the ballast toward the Amtrak. He pulls out his portable conductor's radio and punches the button to call the Jacksonville AU Dispatcher.

Rock Runner: "CSX AU Jacksonville, emergency!"

AU Dispatcher: "CSX Jacksonville, answering emergency."

Rock Runner: "This is K951, holding at Georgetown on Number One Track, Amtrak was crossing over westbound ahead of us, looks like it derailed, they're all over the ground, there's fire everywhere."

AU: "That's on Amtrak P029, over?"

Rock Runner: "That's correct." There may be another train involved."

AU: "Let me get some emergency help out there, stand by."

Boggs phones the Emergency Communications Center in Rockville (Montgomery County) Maryland.

Montgomery County: "Fire and Rescue Communications, Operator Two."

AU: "This is CSX Transportation out of Jacksonville, Florida. Just had a report of a passenger train derailed, and it's on fire, cars on the ground at a location called Georgetown Junction. Are you familiar with that?"

Montgomery County Rescue: "You're telling me that is a passenger train and there is a fire?"

AU: "I just got a call on my radio from another train…. saying that there was a fire and there were cars on the ground."

Rescue: "OK, we're gonna go ahead. We're dispatching it now. We'll get back to you if we need any more information."

The rear of Don Noble's locomotive is resting against the side of the second Amtrak engine and its ruptured and detached fuel tank is leaking diesel directly down onto two of the switch points and their kerosene-burning "snow pots." As Noble stands up and shakes off the sharp pain in his leg, the rear of his F-40 locomotive bursts into flames.

Grabbing his radio handset, he yells into it, "Emergency! Emergency!" Then he pauses, stops, listens and wonders, *What the hell is that damn noise?*

His engine *alerter* is blasting its shrill alarm.

Noble smacks the touch-off button again and again with the edge of his fist but can't turn it off. He mumbles to himself, "I 've got to get out of this engine."

Then his mind clears. *Where is Joey? Where is my assistant engineer?* Suddenly his conductor's voice blasts through the locomotive console speaker. Ritchie Ruff is screaming, "Call 911! Somebody call 911!"

Noble tries to talk into the speaker, "Ritchie, God help us, I can't find Joey. Come help me. I can't find Joey."

Ruff cannot hear him.

Scott Hodges continues running up the tracks alongside the Amtrak passenger cars with his two-way radio in hand. He can hear the voice of dispatcher Boggs.

"CSX AU Jacksonville, calling K951 Rock Runner, over. Can you give me an update? I can't get a-hold of anybody on 29, over."

Hodges: "They're on fire. They're clearing the people away. Conductors are starting to get people off the Amtrak, over."

Twenty-one

CSX recorder: "At the sound of the tone, the CSXT Standard Time will be 17:41:45" (5:41:45 p.m.)

Within the first minute after the collision, residents in the two high-rise buildings on either side of the tracks at Georgetown Junction inundate the Montgomery County Fire and Rescue (911) System with telephone calls. According to normal emergency procedures, the first call will prompt a staff dispatcher to type critical information about the "incident" into a computer network. That action immediately activates alarm "tones" at the fire and rescue stations located closest to the accident site and broadcasts a brief description, address, and the units that are "first due" (the first fire companies ordered to respond) through the loudspeakers in all of the county's 33 stations.

The Emergency Communications Center in the county seat of Rockville had received the earlier message from the Jacksonville CSX dispatcher and decided to get ahead of the curve by making a direct call to the Silver Spring Fire Station in Montgomery Hills. It was geographically the closest to the Georgetown rail junction, slightly over one half mile.

Lieutenant James LaMay, a trim, silver-haired veteran of twenty-eight years with the department, answers the phone. He and master firefighters Mark Brown and R.W. Evans, are three of the six men on duty. Their older, three-bay firehouse, a community landmark, sits on Seminary Road a block off Georgia Avenue near its junction with the Washington beltway. Rockville tells him that this is a "full box alarm" with an accompanying description that LaMay has never heard before – *a train derailment with fires and known injuries.*

Full-box alarm is a predetermined response to a fire in a specific geographic area. In metropolitan Silver Spring that means four engine companies, two ladder trucks two medic units and ambulances will be dispatched without question. Fire engines and trucks in most of the county's jurisdictions normally carry a "company" of three men – a firefighter, a master firefighter and an officer. It will soon become evident, however, that the scope of this disaster may require more resources than that.

LaMay and Brown get their fire engine and tiller-ladder truck rolling. They have been told to go to 1900 Lyttonville Road. That is the front of a high-rise condominium building called The Park Sutton.

Fire engines are so called because they have always been designed to carry a supply of water and some form of self-powered "engine" to pump it. The ladder-tower truck has a pump that can elevate water from a hydrant up onto a high rise building, but usually no on-board water supply. It is also equipped with several hydraulic ladders. The main one is capable of expanding up into the range of 65 to 105 feet. A tiller-ladder truck is two vehicles hinged together with a "bucket" man sitting far in the back to steer the second section around corners. It carries even longer ladders.

Further south down Georgia Avenue near the District of Columbia line, six other firemen are busy preparing dinner and housekeeping their historic, red-brick Montgomery County Fire Station #1. Steve Jones, a tall and youthful-looking master firefighter with fourteen years' experience, happens to be near the telephone when it rings.

The caller asks him, "Is this where I can report an accident?"

Jones tells him, "No, you should call 911."

The man stays on the line. "Well, I have already tried that, but the line is busy."

Jones' curiosity is piqued. He knows that the only way the 911 lines could be backed up is if there are at least 10 calls coming in at once. He asks the guy, "Where is this accident?"

"At 8600 Sixteenth Street, the Suburban Tower."

The firefighter says, "Is it in the front of the building?"

"No, it's in the back."

"Back in the rear parking lot?"

"No, two trains crashed into each other."

Jones thinks that someone might be joking with him and asks the guy, "Who is this?"

The man begins to give him his name just as the alarm tones in the station sound off. Jones says, "Thanks buddy, we're on our way."

He and Firefighter Paul Hefferin join their other crewmembers on their fire engine and ladder-tower truck and roll out onto Georgia Avenue. They are about three minutes from the scene. On-board Opticon instruments will change traffic lights from red to green with infrared pulses as they move along the streets. Three blocks ahead the men catch sight of a column of black smoke rising in the northwest sky.

Coordinated firefighting using multiple companies has been refined over the past century into a military regimen. Each participating company is trained to assume a slightly different role when it reaches site of the incident. The crew on the first-due engine will drive to the address side and

165

immediately begin suppressing the fire using their on-board tank of water. The firefighters on the first-due ladder truck will split up their company to accomplish two things; connect both the engine and ladder truck to a nearby water hydrant and send men in to find and rescue victims. The companies that come later will approach the scene from the rear or sides.

The officer with the initial, on-site crew will radio back to central command, reporting what he sees at the site and his opinion regarding what total resources will be needed. The central dispatcher then has the option to create an "adaptive," or revision of the initial alarm, to send more equipment and personnel or recall some that are already on their way.

On this day, however, all the years of crack firefighter training and experience in the urban part of Montgomery County seems to be off the table, replaced by a new game with unknown wild cards and high stakes. No one had ever seen anything like this; a passenger train wreck with scope of the catastrophe totally hidden from view. The trains can only be reached by foot, up steep, snow-covered and brush-entangled embankments in the dark.

The Emergency Command Center in Rockville needs some answers. Are there two passenger trains, or a passenger and a freight? What about the possibility of tank cars with toxic chemicals leaking or burning? A hundred thousand people live within a one mile radius. They decide to add a second alarm. That will send four more engines, two more ladder trucks, a hazardous materials unit, an additional rescue squad and more ambulances. After that they will wait to hear the initial site assessment from the first officer to arrive before they consider more men and equipment.

The sheared front-end of the MARC P286 it sitting ninety-three feet past the point of impact. The interior of its cab car is splashed wall to wall with diesel fuel, and the engineer's compartment up front has a small flickering fire - what is left of the initial flash. The diesel on the ground has soaked into the snow, floats on the slush and will not ignite.

Fifteen of the seventeen students and one of the two conductors have survived the crash with relatively minor bone fractures, cuts and bruises. They are all still alert. Two others are critically injured. Michael Woodson, seated directly behind the ragged opening, has lost his lower left leg. It will be found later by firefighters outside the train. Thomas Loatman in the rear of the coach is slumped over with a brain concussion. In the second car, Geraldine Dykes thinks she has a fractured rib. Michael Charissis was bucked around but not hurt.

If the trains had collided directly head on, the impact would have bludgeoned the passengers with an even more terrifying shock, equivalent to something between eight and ten times the force of gravity. Because the MARC cab car caught the face of the Amtrak engine off-center, the monster locomotive sliced into and through only part of the MARC coach and dealt the unharmed passengers a relatively mild blow -- something in the range of two "Gs."

Rodney Crawford is lying on his back in the aisle. Tyrai Boyer, also on the floor, is wedged between two sections of undamaged seats. Damien Benetiz remains crouched down and leaning against the metal wall at the rear of the passenger compartment. He and Jimmy Young struggle to stand up.

Benetiz looks up the aisle toward the front of the car. The interior lights are out and all he can see is an ominous orange glow and white smoke moving back toward him. As he watches, the smoke seems to be changing color from white to black. He senses that a real fire is building. Jimmy Young squats down in the aisle to breathe. He knows that there is some sort of special emergency window near his seat, but his instincts tell him to get as far away from the heat and smoke as fast as he can.

Richard Brown appears behind Benitez and grabs his shoulder. Rodney Crawford, his face spattered with diesel fuel, staggers to where the two are standing and reaches out to Brown for guidance. It is so dark that they do not know who they are touching. The three fall over Jimmy Young crawling in the aisle. Tyrai Boyer jumps to his feet and joins the small crowd at the rear.

The interior rear door of the car is open, jammed into its pocket. Benitez and Young are the first to move through it into the small, metal-shrouded vestibule. The other three follow. The space is half the size of an elevator with locked doors and sealed windows on each side. That is as far away from the smoke and fire as the boys can get. The next coach behind them is leaning so far over toward the downhill bank that the passageway to it is completely blocked.

They are at the end of the line.

Eric Garcia is sitting in the aisle. The smoke above him has rapidly turned downward from the ceiling to the height of the seats. He too starts to crawl toward the back. Kelvin Williams is also on his hands and knees. For a few moments there is a layer of fresh air a few feet above the rancid, diesel-soaked carpet. Everyone on the floor is trying to gulp and hold breaths.

These are the seven students that were either sitting in the rear of the car or made it back there on the conductors' warning or immediately after the MARC train came to a stop. The two pocket doors in the vestibule (exits to the outside) operate electronically on sliding tracks, are locked and have no handles. The incapacitated conductors alone have the only keys to open them.

Inside the vestibule, the students frantically run their hands over the surfaces of the sealed doors and peel at the edges of the windows with their fingers. The right door is tantalizingly open one inch. Seven or eight more inches would be enough for everyone to squeeze out. Because it seems like a little extra effort could make that possible, the door attracts an inordinate amount of their attention and time. The boys strain to pull it open a little further, but the door won't budge. Brown starts kicking the metal surfaces. Garcia joins the other three in the crowded space. He and Benitez hammer on the windows with their fists. Those behind them in the body of the coach start shouting, "Come on man! Open that door! We got to get out of here."

Benitez yells back to them, "The doors won't open!"

Crawford, Boyer and Williams huddle inside the rear of the coach beside the restroom door waiting for their friends to find an escape route. Two more students are making their way toward them. Thomas Loatman, seated only ten feet away, is languishing on the edge of consciousness. Crawford steps forward, shoves Benetiz aside and attacks the doors himself. His strength cannot move it.

The little oxygen remaining in the car is being rapidly displaced by smoke. The boys are on the floor. Their lungs are burning. They are giving up hope. Screams are coming from everywhere. "Help! Help me!" Everything toward the front of the coach seems to be on fire. Brown squats down and cups his hands over his eyes, nose and mouth.

In one last gesture of defiance, Tyrai Boyer rises up into the thick, dark cloud. His clothes are soaked in diesel, his face is covered with heat blisters and his raw lungs gulp for air. He fights the urge to scream, then slowly slides down the sheet-metal wall to the floor beside Brown.

"Richard," he croaks in a raspy whisper. "Man, we're gonna die."

Twenty-two

Damien Benitez, Jimmy Young and Richard Brown remain on the metal floor inside the dark vestibule at the back of the cab car. They have given up trying to open the doors. Benitez feebly raises his head and glances rearward through the black fog. His angle of view enables him to see something that was not apparent before, a dim flicker of light. He crawls over toward it and feels a slight rush of cold air on his face.

Turning around, he yells to the others, "Here it is!"

There, right in front of him, is a small vertical opening between the first and second cars, just large enough to reach the outside. Without the light from the Amtrak-engine fire flickering outside, Benitez would not have seen the gap. And because the second coach pitched over at a considerable angle toward the adjoining cliff, the enormous strain between it and the almost upright cab car ahead caused the large gaskets surrounding the space between them to pull apart.

Brown and Young peer out through the aperture and down at the ground. Young forces his body to stand upright. Benitez and Brown prod him on, "You can do it, man. Go ahead. Jump!"

Young hesitates. "It looks like a ten-foot drop from here," he says. "What if I break my leg?"

Steeling his courage, he falls out and down. Crumpled up on bruised hands and knees in the gravel on the ground, Young draws a long breath of fresh air. Brown and Benitez drop out behind him. Benitez looks back at the smoke-filled cab car and worries about Diana. *She will make it out,* he thinks.

Shaking from the cold, Young and Brown quickly look up and down the tracks between the trains. All they see are dark cars, clumps of jagged sheet metal, dislodged train wheels on the ground and fires in both directions. Young flattens out into the stinking diesel-soaked slush and starts shimmying on his stomach under the adjacent Amtrak mail car. Slush soaks into shirt and pants. His red hands burn from the cold, and he can't stop shaking. Brown follows him. On the other side they stagger to stand up and limp across the second set of vacant tracks toward the wooded cliff. Benitez emerges from beneath the car behind them. Young glances over his left shoulder and sees the Amtrak locomotive leaning over the edge of the embankment. The entire scene around him looks like the end of the world.

Staring down the hill through the trees and brush toward the lighted Park Sutton high-rise, the three boys suddenly realize that they looking at a sheer, thirty-foot drop to the parking lot below. Young sits down and pushes himself over the edge. Plummeting through the snow, he tries to slow his descent by reaching out for surrounding bushes, but they only rip his bare hands. Benitez and Brown follow him.

Jimmy Young hits the bottom of the hill and takes off running at a speed he would later say, "Was faster than anything I have yet to top." Continuing up the driveway past the high-rise building and out onto Lyttonsville Road in a semi-state of shock, he is intent on finding a telephone to call his father waiting for him at Union Station. He knocks on the door of the first townhouse he comes to. A man and woman answer the door and take him in.

Rodney Crawford and Tyrai Boyer tumble into the three boys standing at the bottom on the edge of the parking lot. They too had found the opening. Doubled over with back pain, Crawford can hear his friends still in the car crying out for help. He starts to climb back up the hill.

Richard Brown calls to him, "Where are you going?"

Crawford yells, "I've got to see if everybody's out!"

Elworth Freeman, chief technical engineer for the Park Sutton, arrives behind Crawford at the base of the hill.

"You can't go back up there, son," he says to him.

Crawford keeps climbing, and Freeman moves forward and grabs him around the waist in a bear hug.

Tyrai Boyer stumbles over beside them. In an effort to console Crawford, he says, "Don't worry, man, everybody's going to get off. That fire's too big. There is nothing more we can do. We've got to get out of here, that thing could blow."

Crawford collapses in Freeman's arms and the technical engineer helps him to walk over to the warm Park Sutton.

Kelvin Williams is the next student to make it out of the burning car. Three more, Eric Garcia, James Forbes and William Robertson are behind him. They jump to the ground, crawl under the Amtrak car and slide down the hill. One of them is vomiting. The other two are coughing up black smoke and soot. Residents from the Park Sutton emerge into the back lot with blankets, wrap and walk them to the party room of their building.

The eight remaining Job Corps students; Carlos Byrd, Diana Hanvichid, Claudius Kessoon, Thomas Loatman, Lekeisha Marshall, Ka'ris Rudder, Dante Swain and Michael Woodson, and Conductors James Quillen and Jimmy Major are still inside the coach .

Twenty-three

Joan Barr is a fit, thirty-one-year-old, former emergency-medical technician with the St. Mary's County Rescue Squad in Southern Maryland. She currently works as a U.S. Postal Service letter carrier in Silver Spring. Having completed her deliveries for the day, she begins her hour-and-a-half drive home to Lexington Park, seventy miles south and east of Washington. Heading up 16th Street toward the Capital beltway, she starts passing over the bridge that spans the railroad above Georgetown Junction.

The two tracks there run along an elevated bed under the bridge. On either side of them, wooded embankments drop further down to parking lots behind two residential high-rise buildings. The Park Sutton is the thirteen-story block of condominiums on the north side. Its back overlooks the railroad, and it fronts on Lyttonsville Road. The Suburban Tower is the tall, blue and white apartment structure that looks out onto 16th Street on the south side of the tracks.

Halfway across the span, Barr is startled by an explosion so strong that the concussion jolts her inside the car with the windows rolled up. The low stone wall on the left side of the bridge blocks her downward view from the right lane, but she can see a ball of fire and black smoke rising above it. Her initial thought is that a gas line behind the Park Sutton has ignited. Accelerating off the overpass, she turns left onto Lyttonville Road, pulls into the driveway of the high-rise and continues down the hill into its rear lot.

What immediately catches her eye through the trees is the huge Amtrak engine. It is partially on fire and hanging on the top edge of the hill. Jumping out of her car, she catches the sounds of muffled cries, people calling from the vicinity of the long line of dark baggage cars behind the burning engine. Running, slipping and sliding across the lot through the snow, she yells, "Someone call 911!"

Barr reaches the base of the embankment and pulls herself slowly up the steep, snow-laden incline by grabbing bits of ragged brush and tree branches. Emerging at the top, she looks at the wall of windowless baggage-type cars in front of her. The panicked voices seem to be coming from behind that barrier.

Running down alongside the Amtrak cars, she crawls under one of them and emerges beside the second MARC passenger coach. The doors are sealed shut and have no outside handles. Carefully stepping through the jumble of metal train debris and dislocated tracks, she arrives beside the lead MARC car and stands amazed by the massive breach ripped open in the collision. It is oozing white smoke. The floor of the coach is about the height of her chest. Barr moves to the edge of the opening, rises up on her toes and peers into the void. The silhouette of a person back in the smoky darkness appears behind the wreckage of seats. Barr calls out, "Come over here toward me!" The ghost figure does not respond.

She searches for a way to climb up inside, but a healthy fire in what is left of the engineer's compartment begins creeping back along the line of the opening. Suddenly its flames expand as if someone has thrown a bucket of gasoline on them. They instantaneously fill the area above where she is standing and churn out the blackest smoke she has ever seen. Recoiling backward, Barr drops to her hands and knees and crawls back under the Amtrak car.

The probability that loose diesel fuel would ignite was low. Its flashpoint, or point of ignition, is so high (close to 125 degrees Fahrenheit) that it is very difficult to start it burning. A small flame like a match wouldn't do it. In comparison, the flashpoint of gasoline is minus 45 degrees, and its fumes technically can be ignited in rare instances by static electricity.

The thermal-chemical explosion that erupted from the crushed and short-circuited batteries on the MARC cab car, however, created enough heat to set off the initial "boomflash" at the point of impact and created the small residual fire in the engineer's compartment after the trains had stopped.

That small fire gained momentum on the thin film of diesel fuel covering the interior surface of the lead passenger car and sent a plume of white smoke racing back through the eighty-five foot length of the coach. Less than 45 seconds later, an impenetrable fog of black smoke followed. The lack of emergency interior lights guaranteed that the occupants would not be able to see beyond a couple of feet in any direction.

Jobe Breeden, the engineer operating the MARC P279 ahead of the Amtrak on the road toward Brunswick, is approaching Rockville Station. He knows nothing about the accident eight miles behind him and is startled by the sound of a gasping, squeaky voice coming over his two-way radio. It seems to be saying, "Rick, I don't think I'm going to make it." Breeden realizes that it is Conductor Jim Quillen trying to talk to Engineer Ricky Orr. Maybe Quillen has fallen off his train after opening or before closing the doors at a station stop. Nothing else would make sense.

Inside the wrecked and smoke-filled P286 coach, Quillen and the trapped students struggle to hold their breaths, but their bodies contain undeniable reflexes that force them to continue breathing. Once they suck in their first gulp of carbon monoxide (CO) and soot-laden smoke, they will quickly lose their ability to focus on where they are.

CO does not damage the lungs directly. It is lethal only because its molecules have a 250 times greater affinity than oxygen to bind with hemoglobin. When the two join in the lungs, the CO blocks the ability of the blood to transport oxygen and carries only the CO to the brain. The heart continues to pump life-sustaining liquid throughout the body but the brain cells, extremely sensitive to oxygen deprivation, begin to die as soon as their supply is displaced. This condition is called cerebral hypoxia.

The seven students remaining in the middle portion of the cab car became disoriented almost immediately. Most of them were asleep until the crash. The broken and dislodged seats and large cushions that ended up in the narrow aisle prevented them from maneuvering quickly away from the oncoming smoke and fire. The delay allowed the smoke to silently overtake them.

Everything around them and Jim Quillen is hot and dark and suffocating. By the time Joan Barr arrived, five of the kids and the conductor had not moved more than ten feet away from where they were seated. A few were down on the floor trying to breathe. All had ceased screaming. Two of them climbed over the nearby obstructions, found a window, and started pounding on it with their hands.

Twenty-four

Geraldine Dykes inside the second MARC car remembers feeling the train slow and "stumble" just before she was bounced around "like a ping-pong ball." Her first thought was, *Oh, no, some kids have put some stuff on the tracks, and now we have hit it.*

She is on the floor between the seats and struggling to get up. Her left side and left arm are pulsating with pain.

Looking across the aisle to where she had first taken a seat before moving, she sees that the metal wall of the car there is now protruding at least three feet inside the compartment. The sliding front-pocket door to the vestibule near her is held closed by the final resting position of the coach which is leaning severely to the right. That means that this former exit is totally blocked. Light gray smoke is starting to seep into the car and fill the space around her. Dykes feels an overwhelming urge to lie down on the seats and drift off to sleep, but she manages to shake it off.

Mike Charissis finds himself on the opposite side of the coach from where he was sitting. All the lights are out, and his glasses are gone. He kneels down onto the dark floor and pats around for them.

He calls out to Dykes, "You alright?"

"I'm fine," she answers, "but I think I got some broken ribs, how about you?"

"I can't find my glasses, I've lost my glasses."

Dykes recovers her composure and says in a firmvoice, "OK, kid, there's a fire building somewhere out there. We have got to get out of here."

Charissis abandons his search for his glasses and starts to make his way toward her. Using her left hand, Dykes slowly draws the strap of her purse over her head and around her neck, remembers that she had an umbrella, waves her hand across the seats, finds the thing and places it under her arm. Coughing from the diesel smoke, she pulls herself to a leaning position.

Charissis reaches her, grabs her backpack and helps her climb over the backs of the first few seats. They return to the aisle and start inching their way toward the rear of the car. The passageway is very difficult to negotiate because the entire thing is angled so far to the right. Halfway back, Dykes stops to rest. She points Charissis to the emergency exit window on their left.

"See if you can open that," she says.

Charissis slides across the cushions, presses his face close to the window and quickly reads the instructions. *Looks like if I pull this handle at the top,* he thinks, *it will loosen the rubber stripping and the window will fall out.*

He grips and pulls it with all the strength of a fit, twenty-three-year-old military man. The rubber glazing slowly, very slowly detaches from the upper and side edges, but the window remains firmly in place. Then he spots another handle, a smaller one attached to the glass itself. He tugs firmly on it. The pane does not move. In the remaining flicker of daylight, he reads the instructions again and mutters, "Well, maybe I've got to remove the entire gasket first."

Finally, he gets the gasket out and jerks on the second handle again. The window remains firm. He stands on the seat, places his left foot on the wall and pulls until his face turns red. The top of the window comes loose. He works his fingers into the opening and slowly disengages the pane. The entire process takes a full two minutes and some seconds.

Charissis thinks, *What if the car had been full of smoke and people?*

Thirty-five yards away, Engineer Don Noble frantically continues to look for his assistant engineer. Turning around, he wrestles open the door to the engine room behind him, but the intense fire at the rear of the locomotive keeps him from moving any further that way.

Closing that door, he continues to search around the engineer's compartment, behind the left seat and under the dashboard. Joey is nowhere to be found. The toilet-room door in the front is bent and slightly ajar. With all the remaining energy that he can muster, Noble tugs on the handle until the door opens just enough that he can look inside. He can see that here is not much left except a huge gaping hole in the front of the locomotive.

He thinks, *God, I hope he didn't go that way.*

Michael French, the Amtrak electrician and temporary "mechanical rider" on the second locomotive has sustained a mild concussion but regained fuzzy consciousness. He steps out of the cab on the metal ladder and works his way down it to the ground as the flames on the rear of the head engine, just a few feet away, expand skyward.

Noble also opens the outside door on his locomotive cab and sees French down below wandering around beside the tracks. Despite his broken ankle, he climbs down to the ground, takes the young man by the arm, sits him down on a metal signal-control box and limps back to his burning engine to continue looking for Joey. Halfway up the ladder, he hears Conductor Ritchie Ruff calling up to him from the edge of the embankment below. "Don, get out of there. It's going to blow."

Noble replies, "No, I'm not leaving without Joey."

Ruff regains Don's attention, "We found Joey."

Noble and Ruff walk back along the line of their Amtrak. They come upon two policemen that are holding Joey upright. Ruff had seen his pant leg sticking out of the snow, dug him out and left him with the officers. Noble can see that Joey's head is bleeding and his shirt is shredded. He announces to Ruff, "He's cold. He needs his coat. I'm going back to the engine to get his jacket."

Ruff says, "Damn-it Don, the engine's on fire!"

Noble turns toward the locomotive and says, "Well, it isn't burning in the cab yet. I'll get our grips." A minute later he comes back carrying two small suitcases and Joey's coat.

When he finally finishes opening the coach window, Mike Charissis tosses out his duffle bag and Dykes' backpack. He offers his hand to her.

She says to him, "Honey, you're going to have to help me with this purse. I can't raise my arm."

He gingerly eases the purse strap off her neck, crawls across the seat and drops it and her umbrella out into the darkness. She tells him to go first. He wiggles slowly through the opening until his feet touch the ground.

She calls to him, "Should I come out head or feet first?"

"Feet would work better," he says.

Once Dykes is on the track bed, Charissis picks up their gear and tries to decide what to do next. Should he go get assistance for her, or help her walk? Dykes suggests that he go by himself while she waits and rests. There is a small width of unobstructed ground at the edge of the cliff leading toward the rear of the MARC train, so he heads off in that direction.

As soon as he disappears around the locomotive in the rear, two young men from the Rosemary Village complex climb the chain link fence bordering the tracks and run over to assist Dykes. They are Mike Tuck and Jason Grant, local residents whom she would later call "her guardian angels." They hold her arms and slowly escort her through the snow past the MARC and Amtrak locomotives and down a less steep portion of the hill to the Park Sutton.

Joan Barr crawls through the snow under another mail car and comes up near the rear of the burning cab coach. The lower sills of its windows are eight feet off the ground, and the Amtrak car behind her is very, very close. She looks up and sees palms banging on the glass. In desperation, she picks up a piece of metal off the ground. A man appears beside her. He looks like a civilian from the neighborhood. He cups his hands and hoists her up beside the window. She can see two terrified looking boys inside and whacks on the window with all her strength. She can't even scratch it.

The man lets her down. She moves over to the rear door and starts banging on its flush metal. It and the one behind it on the second car are sealed shut and have no apparent apparatus on the outside to open them.

There is, however, a slight separation in the tall rubber gaskets at the junction of the two cars. It begins just above the height of her head. She looks up, but all she can see is black smoke pouring out of the darkness within.

The massive opening in the side of the MARC cab car and the hundreds of gallons of diesel sprayed on the seats inside supplied the initial small, smoldering fire with enough oxygen and fuel to slowly move it to a free-burning phase similar to an outdoor fire expanding in a pile of loosely stacked lumber.

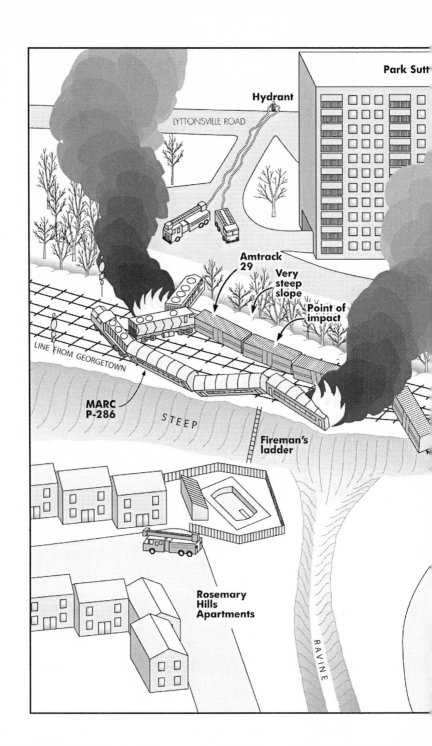

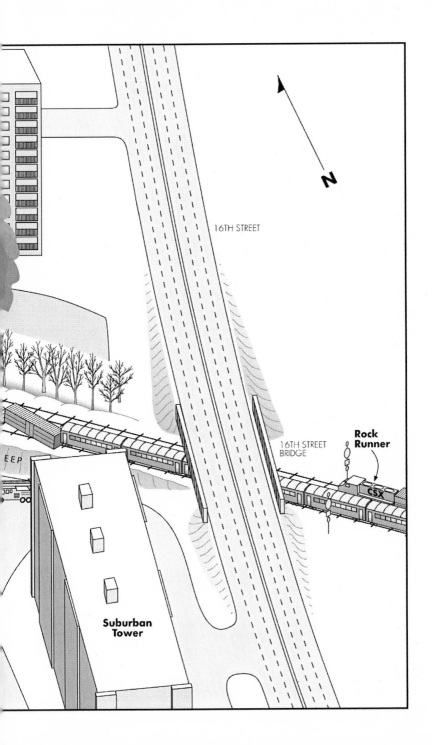

N

16TH STREET

16TH STREET
BRIDGE

**Rock
Runner**

CSX

**Suburban
Tower**

EEP

Outside, that fire's smoke and gases would quickly dissipate into the atmosphere.

A well-fueled combustion within an enclosed space such as a train car or a room in a building, however, will move into an intense second phase so fast that firefighters are trained to anticipate its development, ignore the limited security of their superb protective gear and get the hell out of the small area within seconds (such as diving through a window), or die.

In the case of the MARC car, when the gases from the initial blaze rose upward, they were blocked by the ceiling and turned downward along the walls. This intensified the fire as the available diesel fuel on the seats created ten times more energy than the decomposing cloth and plastic. Both the fuel and the gases rapidly moved the temperature of the fire into the range of 1,500 degrees Fahrenheit. Over the course of a few minutes the heat rose so fast that it converted every flammable object in the car into fuel. At approximately 5:46 p.m., a spontaneous, inferno called a "flashover," raced the entire length of the coach and annihilated everything beyond recognition.

Joan Barr is startled by a loud roar from inside the coach. Flames leap out of the opening above her.

The hands of the students are gone from the windows.

She crawls back under the Amtrak cars.

Twenty-five

5:46 p.m.

Lieutenant LaMay and Mark Brown arrive at the front of the Park Sutton with their fire-engine sirens blaring and truck lights flashing. LaMay spots a curb-side hydrant across the street and stops while a crew member jumps out of the engine cab, runs around and pulls the end of a supply-line off the back. The balance of the hose will automatically feed out onto the ground as LaMay drives down into the rear parking lot.

Brown is close behind with his tiller-ladder truck and crew. He also pauses on the upper street in front of the high-rise long enough for the bucket man to climb down and pull a hose off their truck. The two firemen on the ground secure the lines to the hydrant, and then one of them places a wrench on the top and "charges" it (opens the water supply).

LaMay has barely come to a stop in the lower lot before his other crewman is on the ground dragging a hose off the engine and up the embankment toward the burning Amtrak locomotive. The line is teeming with a special mixture of water and foam designed to neutralize flammable liquids like diesel fuel. The lieutenant scrambles up into the woods around him looking for any semblance of a path.

Suddenly, a woman appears in front of him and says, "It's a mess up there. I'm the manager of the Park Sutton. If you need someplace to treat the injured, you can use our party room." LaMay asks her to go down and give that information to all the emergency medical people who will be arriving in the parking lot.

On the elevated railroad-track bed, he finds two local residents and a policeman standing near the burning engine. The officer says that he heard people screaming from what seems to be another train out of sight behind the Amtrak cars, but he couldn't figure out how to reach them. The second Amtrak locomotive has rotated sideways across the tracks and blocked the view and access to the MARC coaches.

LaMay hurries back down the hill, finds Mark Brown and tells him about the cries. Brown, described by his superiors as "a rather aggressive fellow who loves to go at it," grabs his forcible-entry tools, a flat-head ax and Halligan bar, and starts climbing up toward the jumble of railroad cars. The Halligan, with its claw-wedge blade and tapered pick is an ideal device that one can use to snap open any kind of locked door.

Firefighter R.W. Evans takes a chainsaw off the engine and begins cutting a make-shift trail through the brush for fire hoses and possible evacuation of victims.

Steve Jones from Station #1 on Georgia Avenue pulls his engine alongside LaMay's. His colleague, Paul Hefferin, has taken his station's tower-ladder truck to the Suburban Tower apartment building south of the tracks. Hefferin waits for the police to move the crowd of curious bystanders before he can make his way down into the lower parking lot. From there he can see the front of the burning MARC train some 200 feet ahead of him up the steep hill.

Like Mark Brown, his mission will be search and rescue. Hefferin stops his truck, climbs out, pulls on his "turn out" firefighting gear and straps a SCBA (self-contained breathing apparatus) tank onto his back. With that extra 60 pounds, he will have a tough climb through the snow to reach the MARC cab car.

Distant sirens from every direction are closing in on the 16th Street Bridge and Georgetown Junction. Another two dozen firefighters and emergency medical people are riding and listening to their radios, straining for a clue of what to expect when they arrive.

Lieutenant LaMay climbs back up the hill to the tracks, activates his hand-held radio and starts broadcasting his initial situation report. He knows that the tone of the voice he uses will be as important as the text of the message.

It is measured, precise and calm. He explains that he sees a complex, major incident involving two passenger trains with at least two fires. People are hurt and others are possibly dying. The trains are difficult to reach because of deep snow, steep embankments, and rail equipment scattered in every direction. He suggests that arriving units concentrate in the Suburban Tower's lower parking lot and the Rosemary Hills apartment complex.

His broadcast was automatically recorded on the county's audio system and later used in leadership training classes.

Even though the fire on the Amtrak engine is almost extinguished, LaMay knows how bad this is and requests another alarm. That will bring an additional four engines, two truck companies, another rescue squad and several emergency medical service teams – an additional twenty more people.

Completing his transmission, he looks up into the gently falling snow and suddenly realizes that except for the whispering chug chug of the three idling locomotives, he is momentarily standing alone in a dark and silent landscape.

Mark Brown and Paul Hefferin reach the MARC cab car at the same time from opposite directions and come to the same conclusion, no one inside could still be alive. Jim LaMay circles around the three locomotives and hurries down the side of the MARC train. He pauses beside the first two cars and shines his flashlight through the dark windows. There are no signs of anyone in them. The heavy diesel smoke is held close to the ground by the moisture-laden air and makes his breathing labored. Arriving at the back of the MARC cab car, he too is stunned by the intensity of the fire. Three decades of experience has not prepared him for this.

What followed over the next few minutes was a testament to how difficult it would have been for the firefighters, even with their state-of-the-art training and equipment, to enter the locked passenger cars with people alive, but near death inside.

Mark Brown, Paul Hefferin, Jim LaMay and recently arrived Assistant Chief Monte Fitch all peer through the one-inch door opening into the rear vestibule of the burning car and see the silhouettes of two deceased students lying on the floor on top of each other.

Brown inserts his Halligan bar into the small space, but with all his strength he can only pry the door open a few more inches. When he relaxes his pressure, it drifts back to its original position. Because of the angle that the two first cars assumed when they came to rest, the outside emergency "T" bar handle and instructions to release the doors (on the lower part of the car bodies) are hidden in the snow. None of the firefighters have been trained on how to find or use them anyway.

Back near the extinguished Amtrak locomotives, Steve Jones anxiously looks for a water supply to take down to the MARC fire. Grabbing a portable (150 foot) length of folded hose, he connects it to one of the active ones and threads its lead between the MARC locomotive and the third (last) passenger coach. With the help of two other firefighters and a policeman, he starts pulling the heavy water-charged line alongside the derailed commuter train. The going is slow as the men slog through eight inches of snow bordering the edge of the cliff in the dark.

Within a minute and a half they run out of hose and call for someone to bring them up another 150-foot section. While he is waiting, Jones looks down the hill and sees several fire engines and ladder trucks pulling up the narrow driveway inside the Rosemary Hills, two-story apartment buildings below him. Over the next six minutes those firemen will cut through a steel rebar fence at the base of the hill, lay ladders up a the 35-foot embankment and lug a special power saw up the rungs to open a hole in another six-foot-high chain-link barricade at the top.

Brown and Hefferin know that they must find a way to contain the fire inside the cab car. It is already threatening to spread into the second MARC coach and jump across the few feet to the nearby mail and baggage cars on *The Capitol*.

Jones and the two firefighters with him arrive pulling the extended water line. The assembled group quickly agrees that the only way to effectively fight the blaze is to get inside the cab car. Its windows, however, are too high off the ground to climb through, so they decide to try to enter the second car. It is leaning so far towards them that its windows are only waist high. If they can get inside, maybe they can advance a hose forward from one car to the other through the connecting passageway.

Brown slams his ax into a window in the second car. It cracks into a starburst pattern but does not shatter. He then moves up to the second car's vestibule window. After seven or eight furious blows on the special glass, he finally knocks it out of its molding in one piece. Leaning inward, Steve Jones summersaults through the opening and. stands up inside the crooked vestibule. From that point, he can see that the passageway forward to the cab car no longer exists. Except for a space the width of a couple of inches, it is entirely blocked by the rotation of the coach he is standing in.

"I was in the front of the second car," he remembered, "but I couldn't get through to the burning cab car. Then I noticed a hole in the far side of the vestibule that had been created by the collision. It was a rough opening to the outside. Once I had worked my way through it and dropped down onto the track bed on the left side of the train, I saw the separation in the large gaskets at the end of the cab car – the spot that I later learned was the escape route that was used by nine of the students. With considerable effort I managed to pull myself up through the slit. Once I was inside its vestibule, Hefferin started threading me a water line through the small opening in the blocked passageway.

"My immediate problem was I couldn't work in that small enclosed space until I had shifted the two bodies that we had seen on the floor. The so-called safety glass from the window on the left side had fallen inside and melted to form a cocoon around them. It appeared as if they had been trying to open the one-inch gap in the jammed side-door when the smoke overwhelmed them, and they had died within an arm's length of the real opening to the outside.

"When I started working on the fire, the first burst of water I sent up onto the hot metal ceiling erupted into a cloud of steam around me. Even with my safety goggles, I couldn't see anything for about twenty seconds. When that cleared, I continued moving up the aisle knocking down the flames until I had inched my way about a third of the way through the car. Then my flashlight went dead. By that time we had been on the scene for about a half an hour. I sat on the floor and continued to hit the fire on the ceiling with water. Mark Brown came up behind me and gave me his light. It was only then that I realized that I had been sitting on another body."

Jones and Brown continue to work their way forward but get only a few more yards before they run out of hose. A fire company from Takoma Park comes down the aisle to meet them. That crew had advanced their line from the vicinity of the Suburban Tower and fought the fire from the front of the cab car. A firefighter walking on the gravel ballast outside the train discovers a human leg and Ricky Orr's body lying on the ground.

One of the men inside the gutted cab-car calls out to Chief Fitch, "Should we start removing bodies?"

Fitch doesn't hesitate with his answer. "Don't touch any thing," he says, "The National Transportation Safety Board investigators will want nothing disturbed before *they* get here."

Fitch then walks through the car assisted by both a layer of sand that some fireman has thrown on top of the slick diesel water down the aisle and a rope that another man has attached to the exposed metal remains of the seat backs. He makes a sketch on paper to record the final positions of the victims' bodies.

A volunteer officer from a nearby Wheaton, Maryland, rescue unit comes on board and tells Fitch that he knows where the emergency door handles are located inside the car. He finds the panels on the walls, unscrews them and engages the levers inside. Neither lever works. The doors do not move.

At approximately 6:25 p.m. CSX Dispatcher Crawford Boggs, at the suggestion of the assistant chief, voluntarily surrenders the remainder of his AU shift to another man.

The passengers on *The Capitol Limited* were not trapped inside their cars or threatened by smoke or fire. Those in the forward coaches, however, were severely tossed around by the crash, including Conductor Richard Ruff.

As the senior conductor, Ruff initially suggested that it might be safer and warmer for everyone to stay on the train.

But after ten or twelve minutes, one of the local fire department officers overruled him, and members of the Bethesda Chevy Chase, Maryland, Rescue Squad evacuated the passengers, walking them alongside the tracks and down a path to the basement party room of the Park Sutton. Medical teams were setting up shop there to triage and treat those with injuries and trauma. Those who needed advanced care would be transported to one of three local hospitals, including nearby Walter Reed Army Medical Center.

During the first hour following the crash, approximately 140 firefighters, officers and emergency medical people arrived at the site on 18 fire engines, 9 ladder trucks, 9 mobile intensive care units, 6 heavy rescue squads and 3 water trucks.

Joan Barr, the letter carrier and former EMT, remained it the scene until 2 a.m. assisting the medical people, until an arriving U.S. Postal Inspection Service officer deputized her to help him secure the mail cars from vandals. A few of the less well-intentioned neighborhood people had already broken into the Amtrak baggage cars. Barr never made her drive home that night, but reported to work at 7 a.m., covered in soot and reeking of diesel fuel.

In the ensuing confusion, the nine surviving students moved around the Park Sutton building and ended up as guests in the living and dining rooms of many caring residents. Around midnight, rescue personnel went door-to-door on every floor in the thirteen-story building trying to locate all of them.

The work of removing the deceased victims from the MARC cab car was completed at 4 a.m. after a team from the National Transportation Safety Board had finished their initial survey of the scene. The firemen and the EMTs who had reached the site from the Rosemary Hills apartment complex, used ropes and specially designed baskets to lower the eleven bodies down the snowy cliff by hand. This route was out of the sight of the news crews and cameras.

For several hours after the accident, MARC officials told television stations that no MARC passengers had been involved in the accident. Later in the morning, the State Medical Examiner began the process of identifying all of the victims through dental records. This official later revealed that only three, Rick Orr, Jimmy Major and Michael Woodson died as a result of injuries sustained in the impact. The others had been immobilized and killed by the smoke or the fire. The parents of the missing students did not receive any official notification of their loved ones' deaths for *two full days*.

Twenty-six

Willis Henry, the conductor that should have been on the MARC P286 that Friday instead of Jimmy Major later said, "Occasionally on that Brunswick to Washington trip, I would ride up in the cab compartment and talk with the other conductor and engineer, but not often. I usually sat near the back door of the car and occupied myself with something. That week I had a new hand-held, Palm Pilot organizer. Between station stops I would sit and play with it, entering names and phone numbers. It was like a toy. On that late afternoon run back into D.C., we had only one scheduled station stop and usually not more than a couple of flag stops.

"I always had my two-way radio turned on in case the engineer spotted someone waiting on a platform. I also listened to all the chatter on the channel, the other train crews in the area calling their signals and what track they were traveling. It was like reading a book with the TV on; you're not paying direct attention to the sound but you're picking it up anyway.

"Ricky Orr was a very mature engineer. At that point in his life he had really settled down. I'd imagine that the substitute conductor, little Jimmy Major, had some strong opinions about the roster consolidation and the union's response. He had a good heart and was very outspoken on any topic of railroad business that affected the working man. He knew what was right, and if it wasn't, he could find the right people to contact to get it right.

"The three of them, Jimmy and Ricky and Jim Quillen, were upset about the seniority issue. They didn't want to have to train some former Western Maryland Railroad or Baltimore East-End guy to come in and take over their jobs. It would have been unfair. I think that was what they were probably talking about up there in the cab compartment. When I was with Jim Quillen and Ricky Orr on the previous day, they were all stirred up and discussed it all the way back into Washington. I didn't feel like talking about that. It was old business to me.

"My boss said later that he knew that I would have been back by the rear door in the body of the first car with the Job Corps kids, as I usually was on Fridays. "I'd tell them, 'You-all can be cool, make your noise if you want to. But if we get the first regular passenger in this car, y'all have to shut it off.'

"I think they listened to me because I'm black. Most of them were black. I just gently approached them that way. I would tell them, 'Just knock it down when I ask you to.' I suspect Jim Quillen, especially, was leery of 'em. He didn't want to say nothing like that to them, so he just stayed up front."

Henry realized that he would have survived the initial impact sitting near the rear of the car with a key to the nearby exit doors. But then, the doors were operated by battery power and the batteries were smashed and detached from the cab car in the collision. If Henry had been on the train that Friday, he certainly would have tried to herd the students in the middle of the car to the back and attempted to save Jim Quillen and Jimmy Major. In doing that, he may have saved a few more; but it is highly likely that he too would have perished from smoke inhalation.

Twenty-seven

Within ninety minutes of the collision, investigators from the U.S. National Transportation Safety Board (NTSB) arrived at Georgetown Junction, sealed off the area and began gathering critical evidence. It didn't take them long to realize that they were witnessing the aftermath of one of the most horrific railroad catastrophes in recent American history.

The NTSB was officially created by Congress on the first of April, 1967, with a mandate to investigate civil airline crashes and significant accidents in other modes of public transportation including passenger trains. Their mission was to meticulously reconstruct the details leading up to each tragedy, or near-tragedy in some cases, determine its causes and issue recommendations designed to prevent similar disasters in the future.

During its first eight years, the agency relied upon the U.S. Department of Transportation for its administrative support and funding.. Congress changed that arrangement in 1975, however, when it enacted the Independent Safety Board Act. After President Gerald Ford signed it, the law essentially made the NTSB and its 400 employees free to work and express their findings in a forthright manner, independent of cabinet-level federal officials and the political pressures that often surround them,

Since its inception, the Board's staff have conducted well over 100,000 transportation accident investigations and earned an unimpeachable reputation for carefully analyzing each one (usually over the period of a year) before announcing their findings. Because its professional and non-partisan mode of operation is well known, the NTSB is occasionally asked by foreign governments to assist them in solving on of their high profile and difficult transportation accidents. The agency always pieces together the real story and accurately reports it to the public.

Before the end of the month, the NTSB had established eight teams to examine all of the mechanical, electrical and human aspects of the Silver Spring incident. Each of these groups was chaired by an NTSB investigator and staffed by four to eight professionals with some specialized knowledge in railroad operations and accidents. The members were drawn from the ranks of CSX Transportation Inc., the State of Maryland Transit Administration, Amtrak, the Federal Transit Administration, the Federal Railroad Administration (FRA), the Brotherhood of Locomotive Engineers and Trainmen and the United Transportation Union..

The *Track Group* was responsible for reviewing rail and roadbed maintenance records and documenting the line's condition in the vicinity of the Georgetown Junction.

An *Event-Recorder Group* recovered and analyzed the electronic "event recorders" (black boxes) on the two Amtrak locomotives and the older (8-track) magnetic event-tape on the MARC engine. The NTSB technicians successfully "read out" all the information in their laboratory in Washington.

The MARC tape revealed the train's speed at the time of brake application, its traction motor current, brake pressure, the throttle position and distance it traveled from emergency brake application to impact. The Amtrak recorder stored all the same information plus the status of the alerter and pneumatic controls. This team also took measurements of the wheel circumferences on the MARC locomotive to verify its speed and distance data.

The *Mechanical Group* examined the major mechanical and electrical components on the MARC and Amtrak trains to see if both were functioning properly. They also tested the braking systems on the P286 to verify their integrity. This was accomplished by securing data from the undamaged "event recorder."

The *Signal Group* examined a device embedded in the signal box at the Georgetown Junction that confirmed how the dispatcher-operated signal lights there were set. No such device had been installed at Kensington. They also reviewed the recent signal modifications made by CSX when it expanded the block between Kensington and Georgetown Junction.

The *Human Performance Group* looked at the medical and employment records of both the Amtrak and MARC crews as well as pertinent events in their lives over the 72-hour period preceding the accident. They were searching for any clues that may have presaged fatigue, emotional stress or physical impairment. The committee ordered toxicological specimens from the surviving and deceased crew members and submitted them for drug and alcohol analyses.

Part of their mission was to recreate the final minute-by-minute actions of the MARC crew prior to the accident. Even though a voice recorder was not on board (the Federal Railroad Administration and railroad labor unions have always opposed them), the group reconstructed the events from the Kensington flag-stop to Georgetown Junction from interviews with Jobe Breeden, engineer on the westbound MARC P279, and the surviving passengers on the MARC P286.

An *Operations Group* spoke with the crews of the Amtrak *Capitol Limited* and the CSXT freight, Rock Runner, to check their recollections of the signal aspects at Georgetown Junction and any radio transmissions that they may have overheard from the MARC train [neither one had heard anything].

This team also traveled to the CSX operations center in Jacksonville to study all of Dispatcher Boggs' taped radio and telephone conversations. They reviewed company dispatching procedures and any historical records of signal malfunction complaints submitted by train crews on the Brunswick Line.

A *Survival Factors Group* examined both the structural design and operating features of the two trains. Combining those findings with the medical examiner's report, they were able to analyze the chain of physical events that led to the deaths of the victims. This team also interviewed the surviving MARC passengers to learn what they had experienced and how they had escaped. Part of the Survival Factors Group's job was to judge the adequacy of emergency escape mechanisms in the passenger cars and the timeliness of local fire-and-rescue responses.

The *Crashworthiness Group* studied all the damage to the cars, locomotives and the fuel tank on the lead Amtrak locomotive. They selected the laboratories at the University of Maryland as the entity to conduct comprehensive flammability tests of all materials used inside an identical MARC passenger car.

Because of what had happened to the Job Corps students, the Maryland Mass Transit Administration (MTA) quickly made a bold decision. Five days after the accident and well before the NTSB had commented on anything, the MTA announced that it would voluntarily spend $1.5 million to retrofit *every* double-window on *all* of its existing 110 MARC passenger cars with new emergency exits (22 windows in each car). Federal law still mandates only four emergency-exit windows per car, and even today Amtrak passenger coaches still do not exceed that minimum. With that preemptive action, the MTA set a new standard for its fleet of MARC commuter coaches.

On March 12, the MTA also took to heart an early NTSB safety recommendation and volunteered to install easy-to-operate door openers inside the vestibules of all their cars, devices that *did not require* a CSX employee key. Not so many years later, the agency would also incorporate this safety feature and the expanded number of emergency-exit windows into the construction specifications for all of its new passenger equipment.

Since the National Transportation Safety Board can only issue safety *recommendations,* it must rely solely on its powers of persuasion to convince rail operators and the Federal Railroad Administration (FRA) to find a way to implement them. Over its 50-year life, the NTSB has convinced the FRA and other transportation agencies to act on over 75 percent of its suggestions.

Historically, however, the FRA has always been saddled with two conflicting missions, "promoting the safety of American railroads" and "promoting the efficiency (code name for profitability) of railroads." Although it vigorously enforces existing laws, sponsoring *new* regulations proposed by the NTSB is another matter. The FRA's initial response to its recommendations is usually a rejection, followed by the rationale that unless the safety problem is universally perverse and blatant, the agency will not pursue "unnecessary" measures that may create a "financial hardship" for the rail companies.

In 1994, for example, the NTSB formally asked the FRA to start requiring commuter-rail service providers to install inexpensive cab-control signaling onboard their passenger locomotives in suburban city corridors. The least complex of these devices simply continues to remind an engineer of the last signal he has passed while he is traveling through a block.

The FRA responded with the statement, "It is not the government's role to substitute our judgment for the judgment of senior railroad managers regarding matters within their special expertise and responsibilities as corporate officers." It went on to say, "We have concluded that passenger operations have compiled an excellent safety record and that a major federal regulatory effort is not necessary or warranted."

Since most of the FRA's safety efforts focus on the bulk of their annual workload, the hundreds of grade-crossing collisions between trains and passenger vehicles and isolated freight derailments caused by track integrity problems; it initially viewed the MARC-Amtrak accident as a rare anomaly.

But Silver Spring followed another head-on, commuter-rail collision seven days before in Secaucus, New Jersey. One of the two people killed in that "incident" was an engineer who had been working a split night-shift. With back-to-back passenger-rail accidents in the news, the FRA began to feel pressure from the general public to do something.

On March 4, 1996, less than three weeks after Silver Spring, it took the unusual step of issuing Emergency Order # 20. *Note the number 20.* The FRA is over 40 years old, and they have only issued 20 emergency orders.

This lukewarm mandate was directed to all commuter and intercity passenger railroads throughout the country operating "push-pull" configurations *without* on-board and functional cab-control technology. It stated that whenever any of these trains slowed to a speed below 10 m.p.h. or stopped for any reason (even a scheduled station stop), the engineer was then required to continue moving through the balance of the block at a reduced speed (30 mph) while remaining prepared to stop at the next signal.

The crews tried running their commuter trains under the terms of the new order for a week before they began complaining that it was adversely affecting their schedules. Passengers were also widely vocal.

The FRA revised the order. It would apply only in those blocks that immediately preceded a dispatcher-controlled interlocking with its absolute signals and crossovers. That didn't set well with the train crews and passengers either.

Another suggestion from the FRA stated that the practice of scheduling crews on split shifts should be carefully and immediately re-examined. At the same time, The New Jersey Transit Authority, with its recent incident involving a fatigued engineer, decided to permanently abolish that form of work assignment.

Within a month of the Silver Spring incident, the NTSB deposed (privately interviewed on the record) thirty-one individuals, CSX and State-of-Maryland railroad officials, CSX and Amtrak engineers, conductors, surviving passengers and emergency fire-and-rescue personnel. Following that, the board held three days of open public hearings on June 26th, 27th and 28th, 1996. At those sessions, members extensively questioned twenty-six individuals; (some for the first time and some for the second time) technical experts, CSX employees, surviving victims and professionals from the Montgomery County community that participated in the aftermath of the disaster.

Since the results of the NTSB's investigation would not be released for at least twelve months, the public and press began speculating about the cause of the accident. They generally concluded that the MARC crew had somehow missed or forgotten the yellow, slow-down signal that was reported to have been posted just before the Kensington station.

Engineers and conductors within the Baltimore Division, however, uniformly held Ricky Orr, Jim Quillen and Jimmy Major in high esteem and refused to believe that their three colleagues, with a combined service record exceeding three quarters of a century, could have made such a simple mistake. There must have been another reason. Theories ranged from an operational error at Jacksonville CSX to a signal light or mechanical failure that was covered up by the company.

One of the circulated stories claimed that the P286 crew had been the victim of a "false-proceed" signal, meaning the lights at Kensington were actually green instead of yellow. Every senior engineer has a few career memories of blithely passing a green signal at full speed only to be shocked with a red one at the entrance to the next block. Almost all of them were lucky, another train was not ahead of them on the same track, and they ended up bringing theirs to a halt without serious consequences. Nationwide, CSXT reported 13 rare instances of false-proceed signals in 1994 and five in 1996.

In the Silver Spring case, the false-proceed accusations implied one of two things: either the dispatcher did not realign the switches at Georgetown Junction until after the P286 had passed Kensington (which would mean the crew actually saw a green signal there), or the wayside signal malfunctioned and displayed green lights.

Actively malfunctioning signals (not dead bulbs) come in two varieties, "dropping" signals and "pumping" signals. They both refer to a similar deficiency. The first describes lights that change from green to yellow or yellow to red right before an engineer's eyes, and the second is a constant rotation (pumping) from one color set to another.

On March 13, 1996, only weeks after the accident, three different train crews reported that the east-bound signal at

Kensington was pumping from a clear indication to "stop-and-proceed." These crews each contacted the dispatcher and were told that it was not showing-up on his Jacksonville console. Between August, 1995, and February, 1996, CSXT incident reports stated that there had been 134 signal malfunctions on the line between Washington, D.C. and Brunswick. Almost all of them were caused by either snow, lightning, heavy rain or erratic commercial-power outages.

On February 28, 1996, less than two weeks after the accident, a small and short-lived firestorm was ignited at a hearing before a panel of Maryland state legislators. Leroy Jones, a local union vice president, disclosed that a spiral-ring notebook placed in the crew room at the Baltimore Riverside Yard for engineers and conductors to log their personal experiences regarding signal problems, had since mysteriously disappeared.

CSXT Regional Vice President, Stephen Thienel, publicly denied the existence of such a notebook. Two days later, CSXT officially retracted his statement and conceded that Paul Rahn, the supervisory company engineer in Baltimore, did actually keep an "unofficial" log as described, but that he had not seen the thing since before Christmas.

Vice President Jones stated that the disappearance of the book was not as important as the company's denials. His final comment was, "It leads us to wonder what else we don't know."

And then there was the minor controversy surrounding CSX Transportation's inscrutable *Operating Rule #269*. Six years after the accident, a freight engineer emphatically explained his understanding of it to me in these words:

"That rule," he said, "exempted Ricky Orr's passenger train from having to continue at a reduced speed through the block after he had stopped at the Kensington station." The man was not only wrong; he was not alone. Evidently a few other engineers may also not understand the rule's wording. It is fair to say that the wording could be misinterpreted.

Though the text is poorly written, its purpose is to govern the actions of freight and passenger engineers when they start moving their trains after a temporarily stop within a block.

The following is a verbatim quote of Rule #269 followed by a translation for all who are willing to read it, and maybe reread it, cold sober.

It begins:

"When a train has passed a signal permitting it to proceed without restrictions [a green light] and it happens to stop within the block, the engineer must continue at a reduced speed and remain prepared to stop at the next signal. This must be done until he can see that the next signal permits him to again proceed.

And it goes on to state:

"This rule does not apply to passenger trains making a station stop."

Some railroaders will argue that the exception permits passenger trains to stop at a station and then continue to the next signal at the maximum rate of speed *under any condition*.

The rule does not say that. What it says is - all trains, *all of them,* must continue to obey a slow-down, *restrictive* signal (yellow-lights) throughout the entire block, even if they stop their train for some reason.

On the other hand, the rule differs for passenger trains and freights that receive a "proceed," or green signal, at the entrance to a block and then encounter a delay within it. In that case, freights and passengers are instructed to follow two *different* courses of action when they start rolling again. Freights must move cautiously forward at 30 mph all the way to the next signal, while passenger trains can continue at the full authorized speed.

The rule assumes that a freight train will often be delayed long enough for the signal aspect at the other end of the block to change while a passenger station stop is usually brief enough to be insignificant (usually about one minute).

Two conductors speculated that the adverse weather conditions at the time of the accident may have impaired the MARC's air-brake system during Ricky Orr's final emergency application. One of them postulated that an angle cock could have been clogged with ice. Angle cocks are the control valves (like water spigots) on the ends of each car that are connected by hoses to the angle cock on the next car and used to cut off the flow of compressed air from the engine when an adjoining car is decoupled from the rest of the train.

In theory, if an angle cock on the P286 had been partially blocked, that would have slowed the rapid movement of air from the locomotive's main reservoir through the brake line after the Kensington stop, delayed the recharging of auxiliary reservoirs on one or more of the coaches and diminished the MARC's braking power as it powered down into Georgetown Junction.

The other conductor said that ice could have built up on the brake pads of the P286's coaches and increased that train's stopping time.

Over the many weeks following the accident, numerous Brunswick Line railroad crews performed their own "studies" approaching Georgetown Junction in MARC commuter trains. All of them found that they had no problem bringing their one-engine, three-car units to a full stop ahead of the crossover *without* using emergency braking.

On July 3, 1997, fifteen months after initiating its investigation, the NTSB released its "Railroad Accident Report." The following is the format the agency uses to present its final reports.

- Its investigation "findings," followed by
- Its "conclusions" about the causes of the accident, and
- Its "recommendations" on what actions should be taken to prevent similar accidents in the future.

The NTSB began its 145-page report with the following findings. Only the most significant ones are listed [some with author inserted comment for edification].

The equipment on both trains, including their braking systems, functioned as designed.

The CSX Jacksonville AU dispatcher properly performed his job.

Neither the three MARC P286 crewmembers nor the two engineers and two conductors operating the Amtrak *Capitol Limited* locomotive were physically or mentally impaired. They were all in good health, demonstrated no evidence of fatigue or substance abuse and were highly experienced and qualified for their duties.

The weather did not impair the ability of the MARC crew to see and understand the aspect (yellow, slow-down lights) of the Kensington signal, and the systems at both Kensington and Georgetown Junction operated properly.

The MARC train's engineer apparently forgot the aspect at Kensington which required him to reduce his speed and remain prepared to stop at Georgetown Junction. That was, in part, due to interference caused by performing an unscheduled station stop between the approach signal prior to Kensington and the stop signal at Georgetown.

The conductor and the assistant conductor, standing in the cab compartment of MARC P286, appeared to have not effectively monitored the engineer's diligence and taken action to ensure his safe operation of the train.

Had the FRA required the recording of the MARC P286 crewmembers' voice communications [a discussion of the seniority roster?], it would have assisted the NTSB in their investigation.

If the FRA and Federal Transit Administration (FTA) had required CSX Transportation (as part of the federal grant given for signal modifications) to perform a *Failure-Modes and Effects Analysis* and *Human-Factors Analysis* before relocating signal #100 near Kensington, this accident may have been prevented. [CSX had an adequate staff of professionals in Jacksonville to address such subjects.]

If the Brunswick Line had had the infrastructure in place to utilize the cab-signal equipment already present in the MARC locomotives, this accident may not [most likely would not] have occurred.

The emergency egress of passengers was impeded [totally blocked in this case] because the MARC cars lacked quick-release mechanisms available to passengers on its exterior doors and emergency lighting along the aisle passageway. The absence of comprehensive federal safety standards for passenger cars permitted this to happen.

The catastrophic rupture of the Amtrak locomotive's diesel tank in the collision with the MARC cab car released fuel that sprayed throughout the interior of the passenger compartment and caused the smoke, fire and death of at least eight people.

Because the MARC cars had been fitted with interior materials that did not meet specified performance criteria for flammability and smoke emission characteristics, the safety of passengers could be at risk [the fumes from burning seats can kill you].

The MARC train engineer's use of the reverser during the emergency-brake application resulted in a marginally increased stopping distance.

CSX Transportation and the Maryland Rail Commuter system lacked comprehensive safety oversight to ensure the safety of the commuting public.

The Verdict

At the end of their exhaustive year-long investigation, the NTSB reported its final, considered opinion, a verdict of sorts. There were TWO PROBABLE CAUSES of the accident.

"The First was the apparent failure of the engineer and train crew on MARC P286, because of multiple distractions, to operate their train in accordance with clearly posted signal indications [operator error].

"The Second, and equally important, cause was the failure of the Federal Railroad and Federal Transit Administrations, the State of Maryland Mass Transit Administration and CSX Transportation, to ensure that a comprehensive human-factors analysis was conducted for the Brunswick Line signal modifications (at Kensington). This could have identified flaws in the design that significantly compounded a simple incident of human error [into a major disaster].

"If the above mentioned organizations had provided a redundant safety technology such as available cab-control signals, that simple system would have compensated for human oversights, and most likely prevented the collision."

These findings and conclusions were followed by a number of formal recommendations that were addressed to public and private entities involved in commuter rail operations and safety. While most were specific to this incident, some reiterated long-standing and previously stated rail-safety suggestions made by the NTSB to the FRA and FTA that had not been implemented. The principal recommendations are listed below, followed by the FRA's responses. If you are a rail commuter, you may find the responses very interesting.

The railroad operators should;
- Install voice-recording devices for exclusive use in accident investigations.

The FRA argued then, and continues to argue today, that the process of implementing any such requirement for voice recording would be difficult [the unions oppose them] and would divert attention from other safety priorities."

The railroad operators should;
- Conduct a human-factors analysis for all signal system modifications [not done in the relocation of the Kensington signal].

First rejected by the FRA as "a highly burdensome and subjective exercise;" the agency later accepted it as part of their requirements for federally funded transit projects.

The railroad operators should;
- Require installation of easily accessible, quick-release mechanisms [on the inside of passenger cars] adjacent to exterior doors that will manually open the *outside* doors.

The FRA rejected this requirement for commuter trains, using the rationale that a passenger could use it to open a door and jump off.

Well before this FRA response, however, the Maryland Mass Transit Administration (MTA) decided to install such emergency escape mechanisms on all of its MARC coaches. [Not a single passenger in the ensuing 14 years has used one to open a door and jump off a moving train].

<u>The railroad operators should;</u>

- Require installation of emergency-lighting fixtures that are linked to a self-contained and independent source of power,

"Good suggestion," the FRA responded, but it would insist that such improvements only be required in new coaches manufactured in the years beginning in 2002 (five years from the time of their response).

<u>The railroad operators should;</u>

- Promptly require an inspection and maintenance cycle to test the operation and performance of ALL emergency-exit windows.

The FRA agreed in principle, but limited the inspection to a "representative sample" of windows. They rejected the idea pioneered by the Maryland Mass Transit Administration to expand the number of required emergency-exit windows per car beyond four, or eight for a double-decker coach.

<u>The railroad operators should;</u>

- Immediately perform a comprehensive inspection of all commuter-passenger cars to independently verify that the interior materials used meet the performance requirements for flammability and smoke emissions.

The FRA agreed that all new passenger coaches placed into service after September 9, 2002, must meet such standards. The railroads, however, could be "allowed to test older equipment and make *their own decisions* about relative and acceptable flammability and smoke-emission risks." [Many of the older passenger coaches identical to the ones in the 1996 accident, were still being used to transport passengers thirteen years later].

The NTSB's most far-reaching recommendation, the one that it had placed on its no-brainer and sacred "Ten Most Wanted List" of most important safety improvements for *all* forms of transportation, was the one it felt could prevent all trains from colliding in the future.

- Implement, in the short-term, "Positive Train Control" (PTC) systems for all trains where commuter and intercity passenger railroads operate. Until a [cost efficient] PTC system is available, those rail-service providers should be required to install cab signals, automatic train stop (ATC) or positive train stop (PTS) systems.

This is what the NTSB was talking about:

When an engineer passes a restrictive (slow down) signal, the most basic form of interior locomotive cab signaling will continue to remind him of that fact all the way through the block. Those are the cab control signals currently used on the MARC Penn Line.

A more sophisticated version is called Automatic Train Control (ATC) or Continuous Cab Signaling. It is capable of electronically transmitting up to nine different signal-aspects through the rail into the locomotive and onto the engineer's console. A visual display gives the operator instantaneous, "real-time" information regarding *both* the signal that he has just passed *and* the status of the *next* one ahead.

If the engineer is running under a restricted speed limit, ATC will audibly inform him the second his train is traveling too fast. If he fails *to acknowledge* that warning, the system will apply his brakes. The limitation of this system is that the engineer must only confirm the warning by pressing a button. If he hits the button, but ignores the warning by continuing to speed, the ATC will not stop his train unless it runs a red signal..

The third technology, Positive Train Stop (PTS), is a more intelligent speed-enforcement apparatus. Designed not only to warn an engineer when he is going too fast, it will also give him a braking profile. If he does not follow the profile, the PTS processor will automatically slow or stop his train.

The important distinction between the two is the fact that the ATC will stop the train *after* it runs through a red signal while PTS will stop the train *before it gets there*.

Amtrak now uses both of the these technologies along its 198 miles of Northeast Corridor tracks for passenger trains and freights and has plans to similarly equip an additional 410 miles of its lines. Similarly, the New Jersey Transit system has installed ATC on 82% of its railroads and supplemental PTS developed by the Union Switch & Signal Company on most of their Northeast Corridor trains. The entire project covers 540 miles of their tracks. New Jersey now boasts that they operate the safest commuter railroad in the United States.

POSITIVE TRAIN CONTROL (PTC) uses the PTS technology, but its upgraded forms can also add a digital network and the Nationwide Differential Global Positioning System (GPS) to track each train within the accuracy of a few yards. An extension of this technology is capable of linking all the wayside signals, switches and at-grade crossing gates to a central command center and increasing track capacity to 25%.

The FRA did not embrace the idea of requiring *any* form of cab signaling or automatic braking mechanisms. Its response was, "It is important that we avoid any burden on providers that would result in service cutbacks and diversion of passengers to less safe forms of transportation." [What does that mean? Driving a car?]

The agency did, however, approve the funding a long-range project designed to demonstrate PTC technology on a national level. On February, 13, 1998, almost two years from the date of Silver Spring, the FRA announced its plans to conduct a four-year PTC demonstration for freight and passenger service on a 123-mile segment of a Union Pacific Railroad Line between Springfield, Illinois and Chicago.

The American Association of Railroads voted to invest $20 million for the project, and the FRA and Illinois Department of Transportation (IDOT) agreed to contribute $14 million. In 2000, IDOT awarded a $34 million contract to the Lockheed Martin Company to implement it.

By 2004 they had proved that Amtrak passenger trains could safely run at speeds up to 110 miles per hour, reduce their travel time between Chicago and St. Louis by approximately one hour while increasing both line capacity and fuel savings for freights. As a result of this successful demonstration, the FRA announced new PTC standards on March 8, 2005, but refused to recommend legislation that would require any U.S. railroads to install them.

Afterwords

The NTSB investigation effectively debunked the signal-failure speculations some professional railroaders firmly believed. The "false proceed" theory postulating that the P286 had a green signal at Kensington was refuted by hard evidence. The NTSB not only inspected the Kensington signal but sealed the Georgetown Junction signal-box on the night of the accident and later tested its totally undamaged electronic signal data recorder. While located at opposite ends of the same block, the two sets of signals were electronically linked to each other. Everything within the system tested normal.

The NTSB also confirmed that the crossover tracks at Georgetown had remained "reversed" from 4:33 p.m. to the moment of the accident (over an hour). Both those findings meant that the lights at Kensington were yellow well before the MARC P286 arrived.

In every one of the 134 signal-malfunction cases recorded in CSXT incident reports between August 1995 and February 1996, the signals had immediately reverted to a fail-safe mode by either displaying a yellow aspect or going blank. None had shown a green light.

The NTSB's official time-and-motion studies used MARC locomotive and car equipment that were virtually similar to the P286. The investigators found that Engineer Orr's train decelerated as fast as was physically possible once he had applied its emergency brakes. The agency also verified the MARC's speed at time of brake application, the distance over which it traveled to impact, its running weight and its optimum braking capacity. This ruled out the possibility that accumulated ice on its brake pads or inside an angle cock had diminished the train's ability to stop.

And, even though the "sanders" on the P286 (devices positioned above and ahead of the engine's wheels to spray sand on the tracks) were clogged shut, the NTSB determined that sand would have been an insignificant factor in assisting the train to stop at the speed it was traveling.

The Brunswick Line crews who claimed they could bring their three-car passenger trains to a stop well before the Georgetown Junction signal overlooked one thing. The reality of February 16 was that Ricky Orr traveled almost a hundred yards past the point where the stop-signal was first visible before he applied his emergency brakes. The scene ahead at the time took him and the two conductors completely by surprise. The data clearly proved the fact that he briefly hesitated before applying the emergency brakes.

Tom Vanderbilt, author of the recent book, *Traffic,* repeated a point made by noted traffic researchers. They said, "It takes us longer to process the fact that a car is approaching in *our* lane on a two-lane highway instead of, as we would expect, in the *other* lane. That 'second look' we colloquially say we take when 'we can't believe our eyes' may be a very real and time-consuming effort."

The NTSB's analysis of the P286 black-box data confirmed the maximum distance from which the signals could have been seen by the engineer and conductors, the exact time the emergency brakes were activated, the time of the collision and the speed of the MARC at each point.

From that, they mathematically deduced that the train advanced 290 feet at 65 m.p.h. (three seconds) past the initial point where an engineer could have first caught sight of the red lights. The crews that later tested their trains' stopping power most likely maintained their vigilance around that final curve and began braking as soon as the signal came into view.

Russell Bly, the only member of the of "The Crew" not present on the death train, still got angry years later when he thought of the Amtrak engineer's decision not to slow down. If Don Noble had reacted like Ricky Orr and gone into full emergency, the two trains would have collided directly head-on at a combined rate of speed not very much different (67 m.p.h. instead of 70).

The lead Amtrak engine, with its overwhelming height and preponderance of weight most certainly would have both entered and telescoped the cab car, crushing everything in its path for a considerable distance. That too, would have been deadly for the Job Corps students, Engineer Orr, Conductors Major and Quillen, and probably Don Noble. A direct hit also would have ruptured the Amtrak fuel tank, but not sprayed its contents throughout the passenger compartment.

The final, most popular and persistent belief held by many railroad employees in the Washington area claimed that propane-fired switch heaters (instead of simple kerosene snow pots) were in use at Georgetown Junction to keep the switches operable at the time of the accident and caused the intense fires after the trains collided.

That was not true on two counts. First, kero is a more complex hydrocarbon that ignites with more difficulty and *burns at a higher temperature than propane.* Think this - diesel very hot, kerosene hot and propane cooler.

Secondly, investigators never found any propane tanks of any description on the site. The aerial photograph of the sealed-off area, taken for the NTSB on the morning following the accident, confirms that propane tanks were not there. Sixteen, working kerosene snow pots, however, were present under the switches.

The controversial CSX consolidated roster that may have consumed the attention of the MARC crew on their way back to Washington that Friday never amounted to the personnel disaster that the men feared. In retrospect, Orr, Quillen and Major would have advanced their seniority positions in the small (protected) fraternity of passenger service. In the end, no one from outside of their district could have bumped them. When the consolidation was completed several months later, Russell Bly moved up 40 turns.

Don Noble, the gentle bear with a caustic sense of humor, died suddenly of a heart attack on May 23, 1999. He was only 53 years old. His wife and four children stayed in Middletown.

Joe Ruff was at home on temporary, disability leave when he struck it rich in the Pennsylvania lottery. He began traveling with his wife and fishing.

Joey Fratangelo took a permanent disability pension and did not go back to railroad work.

Joan Barr is still employed by the U. S. Postal Service but has transferred from Silver Spring to a location near her home in southern Maryland. On September 25, 1996 the Association of Letter Carriers selected her as its National Hero of the Year, the first woman ever to receive that honor and a modest $500 award from the 318,000 member union.

The multi-billion dollar CSX Company and MARC, on the other hand, refused to reimburse the expenses that she personally paid for post-accident psychological counseling, claiming that her attempted rescue actions were voluntary and not part of a job. So it goes.

Secretary of the Navy, John Dalton, presented Michael Charissis with the Navy and Marine Corps Medal on April 26. 1996.

In the days following the wreck, the surviving students and their families were aggressively pursued by reporters, television crews and lawyers. Jimmy Young left his home and went into hiding at his brother's house to escape them. He and some of the other students said that they were more traumatized by the press and attorneys stalking them than the accident. Kelvin Williams was so leery of strangers inquiring about his welfare that he retained a local lawyer to answer questions on his behalf.

Four of the surviving students; Jimmy Young, Kelvin Williams, James Forbes and Richard Brown returned to the Job Corps Center at Harpers Ferry and finished their studies. They are all currently employed. Young, a shy, well-spoken and introspective young man would like people to remember what happened. For years, he drove to Silver Spring on the anniversary date of the accident and walked the tracks at Georgetown Junction.

Immediately following the accident, mid-level officials at the U.S. Department of Labor (DOL) in Washington instructed senior Harpers Ferry Job Corps managers to plan and schedule a memorial service for Friday, February 23, just seven days after the accident. Deputy Center Director Jennifer Mobley remembered the central office people telling her, "We are going to do this while the cameras are still rolling."

She and other staff members at the Harpers Ferry Center believed that headquarters was trying to transform the occasion into a national media event to showcase the Job Corps program. They pleaded for a postponement of the service until the surviving students had had enough time to privately grieve for, and bury their friends. Seven of the eight students killed in the accident were not scheduled to be laid to rest in their communities until after that date.

Washington DOL then stepped in and took control of the function, directing local Harpers Ferry employees to line up students to clean buildings, cook for the arriving guests and park their cars. Several invited dignitaries, including Secretary of Labor, Robert Reich, heard about the discontentment and declined to attend. No one at the Department of Labor even asked any of the nine surviving students to participate in the ceremony.

Center Director Claude Thomas and Residential Living Manager Joseph Johnson, both career employees, were transferred to other locations several weeks after the last young victim was buried. Deputy Director Jennifer Mobley remained on the campus as the highest ranking manager but was not elevated to acting director. Instead, Washington dispatched other DOL employees to Harpers Ferry to operate the center on a temporary basis. Months later, Mobley, too was reassigned out of the area. She eventually left the agency to work for another federal department.

Since 1996, the Department of Labor has contracted most of the facility staffing to a private company called ResCare. A few jobs are still held by career public-service individuals, but most of them, the ones that originally signed up for reasons not related to salary, have departed, convinced that the contractor does not exhibit the same intense commitment to the students that they had.

The Mayor of Harpers Ferry at the time, Walton (Kip) Stowell, took it upon himself to design a simple, "living" memorial on the grounds of the campus. Today, on a small spot in an elevated field just outside of the facility's front gate, a circle of eleven weeping cherry trees shade an equal number of inscribed park benches. The southeast portion of the circle remains open in the general direction of Silver Spring. Stowell said that his purpose was to create an outdoor "room," a serene space for contemplation and reflection. Some say the memorial has the general shape of an old-fashioned keyhole in a door.

The Chief Executive and Council of Montgomery County, Maryland, embedded a bronze plaque in the side of the stone wall on the 16th Street Bridge that passes over Georgetown Junction. If you walk out on the bridge you can see that it contains the names of all the eleven victims.

For years following the accident, a group of people in Brunswick organized a reunion for families and friends of the departed crew and student passengers. The date varied, but it was usually held on a Saturday in March. The attendees would first assemble around a small monument down beside the train station. One person would read the eleven names, pausing between each one, while someone else rang the glass-encased locomotive bell after each was called.

Dante Swain, age 18, of Baltimore
Michael Woodson, age 16, of Philadelphia
Diana Hanvichid, age 17, of Woodbridge, Virginia
Lakeisha Marshall, age 17, of Capitol Heights, Maryland
Carlos Byrd, age 17, of Baltimore
Claudius Kessoon, age 20, of Landover, Maryland
Thomas Loatman, age 23, of Vienna, Virginia
Karis Rudder, age 17, of Elmhurst, New York
Richard Orr of Glen Burnie, Maryland
James Major of Linthicum, Maryland
James Quillen, of Frederick, Maryland

Then an engineer would drive a block of three CSXT locomotives slowly past the group and engage his air-horn to emit a long moan. From there, the participants would walk up the street to the Brunswick Fire Department community center, eat lunch and reminisce.

Ricky Orr's parents, Keith and Betty Orr, faithfully attended those annual luncheons. They were the short, thin and distinguished looking couple that usually sat silently at the end of the table.

Leechel Reynolds, the legendary conductor, personally raised the funds to build the bell memorial next to the Brunswick station and laid its three-foot-tall, brick foundation with his own hands. A few years later, he died from the long-term effects of exposure to airborne asbestos in his younger days working in the Baltimore yards.

Russell Bly is still a personable and popular conductor working on MARC passenger trains. His current turn is one of the relatively new runs between Frederick, Maryland, and Washington. Ironically, his father was the fireman on the last B&O passenger train that ran out of that city before the company closed the station in the late 1940s, and Russ was the senior conductor on the inaugural run out of Frederick when commuter service was reinstated there over 50 years later in 2001. He will probably retire this year at age 60.

For Engineer Jack Reed, his 2009 retirement started out riskier than running a coal train downhill in a heavy fog. After the parties were over, he went on a hunting trip, fell out of a tree stand and broke his pelvis and two ribs. When I first interviewed Jack in 2001, we were sitting in an empty MARC coach parked in Union Station. Suddenly the lights went out. I thought that the interview was over, but he continued with the quip, "I have always done my best work in the dark." We kept going.

The parents of the deceased students; Jim Quillen's wife, Betty; Ricky Orr's estranged wife, Linda; surviving students; slightly injured passengers and Amtrak crew members accepted monetary settlements from the CSX and MARC insurers. Settlement language mandated that all of them sign agreements releasing any "claims that they may have against any party for their losses." Those documents also included oaths of silence regarding the amounts of the payments. They all continue to honor those pledges.

Had the wives of the crew members refused the offers and taken wrongful-death claims to court, they would have faced a unique legal precedent that originated with [and how about this title?] the Federal Employers' Liability Act of 1908. Roughly paraphrased, it provides that a railroad employee, or his heir, is entitled to receive only the percentage of a jury award against the company that equals the company's percentage of fault in an accident that injured the employee or took his life. Federal law. Period.

The NTSB determined that CSXT and the Maryland Mass Transit Administration (on one hand) and the P286 crew (on the other) were equally responsible for the crash. If the heirs of the crew members had gone to a jury trial, they would have been eligible for only 50 percent of the money that a jury may have awarded (minus substantial legal fees). Instead of risking that, two of the three widowed spouses took the railroad insurance company's offers.

Peggy Major alone sued CSX Transportation because she believed that the company had not offered adequate financial remuneration for her husband's death, and that he was not responsible for the accident. After nine years of painful litigation, she finally accepted a modest settlement which paid for her son Jimmy's college education and provided him with some startup money. He is now an alumnus of East Carolina University in North Carolina and a successful construction manager working on the Eastern Shore of Maryland. Jimmy, Jr. in turn bought his mother a new compact car.

Willis Henry has already planned his retirement as a travel consultant, but is still working as a conductor on MARC trains traveling between Baltimore and Washington. He declined to mark up for that Baltimore to Brunswick turn again. The run was later deleted from the MARC schedule. Many people still remember the emotional speech that he gave at the memorial service held at the train station in Brunswick after the accident. His "baby" sister, as he calls her, Daisy A. Henry, became an Amtrak engineer.

Conductor Henry thinks he got a "second chance," of sorts. Years after the accident, his Baltimore-bound MARC commuter became disabled and stranded on the tracks as another train was approaching it. Although there was no collision, Henry quickly and successfully evacuated all of the passengers from the lead cars before that possibility arrived.

Jim LaMay and Monte Fitch retired from the Montgomery County Fire Department in 2000 and miss their former profession. In 2003 Fitch accepted a unique offer from the U.S. Department of Defense and deployed to Iraq for six months to train, equip and modernize (effectively rebuild) the fire service there.

Steve Jones is a battalion chief with the Bethesda, Maryland, Fire Department. Paul Hefferlin remained with Montgomery Country and is now a lieutenant. Mark Brown retired after twenty years' service, moved to Phoenix, Arizona area and joined a local police force. Crawford Boggs worked several more years managing another territory from the Bunker as a CSX Dispatcher in Jacksonville, before he retired.

CSX later moved 80 dispatchers from Jacksonville to a new center in Huntington, West Virginia.

Each attendee at the funeral service held for Michael Woodson at the Holy Cross Baptist Church in Philadelphia on March 2, 1996, was given a program bearing the statement, "Always Forgive." It was written by his mother.

Even though investigators most often cite "operator error" as the cause of 80 percent of today's railroad accidents, that general statement always proves to be too simplistic. James Reason, noted psychologist and author of the book *Human Error*, wrote, "Rather than being the main instigators of an accident, train operators tend to be the inheritors of system defects created by poor design, incorrect installation, faulty maintenance and bad management decisions. The engineer's part is usually that of adding the final garnish to a lethal brew whose ingredients have already been long in the cooking."

The simple fact remains that Engineer Orr, conductors Quillen and Major, and eight young men and women would be alive today had a simple backup system been in place inside the locomotive to compensate for "operator error."

The Legacy of Silver Spring and Metrolink

On October 1, 2008, a month before the national elections, the United States Congress passed an amazing, bipartisan piece of legislation, "The Railroad Safety Improvement Act of 2008." (H.R. 2095). It was subsequently signed into law by President George W. Bush.

The law, among many other things, wholly adopted the NTSB's strongest recommendation from the 1996 Silver Spring investigation.

It mandated that within seven years (by 2015), all railroad entities providing commuter passenger service shall implement [meaning "install"] a Positive Train Control system approved by the U.S. Department of Transportation. The law defines PTC as a system "designed to prevent train collisions, speed derailments, incursions into work zones, and the movement of a train through a switch in the wrong direction."

The Department of Transportation is authorized to offer $50 million a year in grants to rail-service providers over the next 5 years to help operators make the transition to PTC

"Authorized" funds are not "appropriated" funds, so the future status of this intention is not yet "money in the bank" for DOT or the railroads.

So, until 2015 or beyond, commuters on the Brunswick and Camden MARC lines, and thousands of other commuters around the country, will be "riding naked" without any backup safety override of an engineer's possible fatal distraction. Over that period, let other people sit in the front car.

The Hours of Service Law was amended to provide that a railroad employee cannot be required to return to duty unless he has had at least 10 consecutive hours OFF DUTY during the prior 24 hours, etc. And, "during a train employee's minimum off-duty period of 10 hours, a railroad carrier and its officers and agents, SHALL NOT COMMUNICATE with the employee by telephone, pager or in any other manner that could reasonably be expected to disrupt the employee's rest." The same applies to a contractor or subcontractor to a railroad carrier, its officers and agents.

The NTSB is hereby authorized and instructed to select an individual from *its* rolls to serve as a "director of family support services" in the event of a rail-passenger accident. That person will be responsible for acting as a point of contact within the Federal Government for the families of passengers involved in the accident. On-board crew members and anyone else injured or killed in a rail accident are considered to be "passengers" under this law.

This director of family services will immediately designate an independent, nonprofit organization with experience in disasters and post trauma communication with families, to notify the families of the passengers, before providing any public notice of the names. This organization will also;

- oversee the emotional care and support of the families, including taking actions to provide an environment in which they can grieve in private;

- meet with families who have traveled to the location of the accident;

- contact those unable to make the trip; and

- arrange a suitable memorial service in consultation with all of those directed affected.

In so many words, the NTSB is also directed to assure that the rail carrier will "provide reasonable compensation [pay the bill] to any organization designated" by the director of family support services.

These final provisions are so blatantly appropriate that they make one smile in the reading of them.

No person or unit of government "may impede the ability of the families of passengers involved in the accident to have contact with one another." [That must have happened in the California Metrolink accident]

"No unsolicited communication may be made by an attorney (or representative of an attorney) or any potential party to litigation, including the railroad carrier, concerning a potential action or settlement offer for personal injury or wrongful death to those injured in the accident or to a relative of an individual involved in the accident, before the 45th day following the date of the accident.

Sources and Credits

1-3   National Transportation Safety Board (NTSB)
supporting documentation for File Number DCA96MR004;
Interviews, public hearings, documents, and reports
by investigators. Page numbers do not transcend the
multiple sections.

4-6   Recorded interview with Willis A. Henry, Sr.,
December 2, 2000, Baltimore, MD.

11   The people who: Recorded interview with John P. Hankey,
August 23, 2004, Savannah, GA.

13   *A History of Brooklyn – Curtis Bay,* 1976, The Brooklyn –
Curtis Bay Historical Committee. Also www.curtisbay.com.

13-26   Recorded interviews with Russell Bly, May 19, 2001 and
January 20, 2007, Mt. Airy, Maryland..

27   Railroad men who: Hankey
After only two years: Bly

28-29   Recorded interview with Jack Reed, August 8, 2000,
Washington, D.C. Union Station.

30-31   Stover, John F. *History of the Baltimore and Ohio Railroad.*
Purdue University Press, 1987.

31   Copy of the Deva McCarter papers provided by
Paul Sorrow, First Vice President, Brotherhood of
Locomotive Engineers and Trainmen, Cleveland, Ohio, 2002.

31   Today a ten: Reed

32   Gamst, Frederick C. *The Hoghead*; An Industrial Ethnology
of the Locomotive Engineeer, Holt Rinehart & Winston, 1980.
Interview with Opha Herdman, Brunswick, GA, 2005.

32-33   Reed

34   McCarter papers.

35-36   Interview with Opha Herdman, Brunswick, Georgia, 2006.

36   Reed

37-38   Trim and muscular: Bly

39-40   Bly

42-44   Stover

44-46   Jacob, Kathryn A. *Mr. Johns Hopkins,
The Johns Hopkins Magazine,* January, 1974.

46-48   Harwood, Herbert H., Jr. *Impossible Challenge;
The Baltimore and Ohio Railroad in Maryland,* 1979,
Barnard, Roberts and Company, Inc. Baltimore, MD.

48   Those far reaching: Stover

48-49 Harwood

52-54 Stover

53   The Capitol's "Martha Washington:" Kratville, William W., *Steam , Steel & Limiteds*, Omaha, NB, Barnhart Press, 1962.

54   Even with that burden: Stegmaier, Harry, Jr. *Baltimore & Ohio Passenger Service 1945-1971, Volume I,* TLC Publishing, Lynchburg, VA, 1993.
Only fresh vegetables: Clark, Michael J. *"Capitol Limited, Now a Page in Rail History," The Baltimore Sun,* May 1, 1971.

54-55 Interview with Winnie Hane, and Amtrak conductor, Brunswick, Maryland, 2002.

55   Stover and Harwood

55   It will be the policy of.: Text on official company brochure, *Exhibit of the Baltimore and Ohio Railroad at the National Antietam Commemoration, Hagerstown, Maryland,* September 4-17, 1937

56-57 Stover

59-62 NTSB docs.

62-64 *The Washington Post* and *The Washington Times,* February 17-18, 1996.

68-70 Harwood

70-72 *The "Y" and How, A Picture Story of Progress, The Brunswick Y.M.C.A.* 1929 (brochure)

72-73 Hane, and Brunswick City Councilman Jim Castle

73-74 Stover

74   Hane

78-79 Linda Noble, telephone interview regarding a description of her husband, 2002.

79-80 NTSB docs.

81-82 Author site visit, Jacksonville, Florida, 2003.

83-86 NTSB docs.

87,89 CSXT transcribed dispatcher voice recordings. NTSB supporting documentation for File Number DCA96MR004

91-92 CSXT voice recordings.

93-95 NTSB docs.

95   Quillen was overwrought: Bly

96-98 NTSB docs.

98-99 The concept of: Wilson, Charles Morrow, *Diesel: His Engine Changed the World,* D. Van Norstrand Company, Inc. 1966.

99-102 Coifman, Benn, *Evolution of the Diesel Locomotive in the United States,* railfan.net, 1994.

Armstrong, John H. *The Railroad – What It Is, What It Does* Simmons-Boardman Publishing Corporation, 1979.

104   When an engineer is preparing: Nice, Karim, *How Diesel Locomotives Work*, Howstuffworks.com

106-108   It has always been: Armstrong trainweb.org/railwaytechnical/sighis, *The Development of Railway Signaling,* Ingham, Craig,, 1999 and *Signals*, The Reading Society of Model Engineers, 1996.

109   Yesterdays block signals. Dennis Mogan, Director of Safety and Rules for the Northeast Illinois Railroad Corporation, METRA. Testimony in NTSB public hearing doc. June 27, 1996.

110-114   Gurner, Bruce, *Casey's Last Ride*, Water Valley Casey Jones Museum. *Casey Jones and Engine #382*, 100 Year Anniversary, NTRAKAGE Issue #129 Casey Jones accident report filed by the Illinois Central Railroad, and transcribed for the Casey Jones Railroad Museum State Park on trainweb.org/caseyjones/report. McDaniel, Amy, *Casey Jones' legend rooted in historical fact, The Jackson* (MS*) Sun News,* December 20, 2001.

114-115   The MARC locomotives: Conversation with Howard Taulton, Amtrak electrician, Union Station, Washington, D.C. 2008.

115   NTSB docs.

116-118   Unionstationdc.com

118   NTSB docs.

120   Author ride on Amtrak P029.

121,123   NTSB docs.

122-124   CSXT transcripts.

126-130   Bentley, John, *An Introduction to Train Brakes,* The Traffic Accident Reconstruction Origin (TARO). technical journal website, 2002. If a brakeman fell: Hankey alaskarails.org train-dynamics.com trainweb.org/railwaytechnical/brake

130   Levine, I. E. *Inventive Wizard: George Westinghouse*, Julian Messner, Inc. 1962.

130-132   Snow, Richard F. *Lorenzo Coffin*, American Heritage.com on-line magazine, 1979.

132-135   train-dynamics.com

138-140   CSXT voice transcripts.

140-161   NTSB docs.

160-161   CSXT voice transcripts

163-166   Recorded interview with Lt. James LaMay and Chief Monte Finch, August 13, 2002,. and telephone interview with Steve Jones, 2002.

166-172   NTSB docs.

174-176   Interview with Jimmy Young, 2003.

176-184   NTSB docs.

185-187   LaMay and Jones

187   NTSB docs.

187-188   Davis, T. Neil, *Flashover,* Article #367, Alaska Science Forum, January 18, 1980.
The Dynamics of Fire Growth, The University of California at Davis, Fire Department website

188-189   Lamay and Finch

189-194   NTSB docs. and
Joan Barr, the letter carrier. Burkitt, Janet, *Southern Maryland Woman* […], Capital News Service article, September 25, 1996.

194   For hours after the accident: *The Washington Times*, February 20, 1996.

195-196   Henry

197-200   NTSB docs.

200-201   Five days after the accident: *The Washington Times*, February 22, 1996.

201-203   NTSB docs.

205   CSX Regional Vice President quoted in Associated Press article printed in *The Washington Times*, March 2, 1996.

206   CSXT Operating Rules.

220   Young

220-221   E-mail and telephone interview with Jennifer Mobley, 2007, and materials provided by Marshall Coleman, former Harpers Ferry Job Corps employee, including articles in *The Martinsburg Journal* (WV) newspaper,

February 17-24, 1996, and *The Washington Post*,
February 18, 1996.

221-222   Interview with Mayor Stowell, 2006.
224   Interview with Peggy Major, Baltimore, MD, 2007.
           and at a Brunswick reunion in 2003.
224-225   Henry
225   Each attendee: Coleman, Program for Michael
           Woodson's funeral.

Acknowledgements

I am gratefully indebted to the following people for their personal recollections and helpful guidance:

Jack Reed, the engineer's engineer, Russell Bly, the gold standard for conductors and Willis A. Henry; without their willingness to share their memories I would not have moved past first base.

The anonymous clerk at the National Transportation Safety Board in Washington, D.C. who proved that her agency is truly the most transparent and forthright in the entire federal government, by providing me unlimited access to the accident investigation files. She did her job well as she was supposed to, but remains anonymous to me only because I never learned her name. I am also grateful to Jim Rosenburg at the NTSB, another public servant in the finest sense of those words.

Richard Dallam, my friend the retired Washington area air traffic controller, for early edits and encouragement..

Conductor Winne Hane and former City Councilman Jim Castle for introducing me to the rich history of Brunswick.

Former Job Corps student Jimmy Young.

Peggy Major and Linda Noble for graciously talking with me about their husbands.

Jim LaMay and Monte Fitch, retired Montgomery County, Maryland, Fire Department officers, who sat with me in the Mt. Airy Pizza Hut one afternoon and poured out their hearts about the accident. And to Firefighters Steve Jones and Paul Hefferin.

Michael Putzel and David Lobenstine, the professional editors who separately looked at immature drafts and emphatically set me straight. Putzel also suggested that I change the title from *A Matter of Seconds* to *Train Wreck*.

Gene Thorp, old, young friend and cartographer with *The Washington Post*, for crafting a map and accident scene illustration from my rough sketches.

My wife of 44 years, Anne Douglas, who accompanied me on several interviews and provided invaluable suggestions.

Corey Sonnecken, our daughter, the graphic artist, for working on the other map, and her husband, Brendan, the Loudoun County firefighter, for technical advice.

Marshall Coleman, former official with the Harpers Ferry Jobs Corps Center, for giving me saved newspaper articles, brochures and his opinion. Thanks also to Jennifer Mobley for her candid thoughts.

John Hankey, former Brunswick engineer and curator of the B&O Railroad Museum in Baltimore, now consultant to the History Channel and local governments trying to preserve and interpret their historic railroad facilities – for his stories, opinions and inspiration. He said this project would take a long time and he was right.

My friend from college days, Paul Sorrow - now First Vice President of the Brotherhood of Locomotive Engineers and Trainmen.

Other lifelong friends that took the time, Donnie James, John Kelchner and Gary Baker.

Author's Note

While I rode thousands of MARC commuter trains from West Virginia to Washington D.C. on the Brunswick Line for over 20 years (about 750,000 miles by rail), I happened to be on the coast of South Carolina, on the day of the accident.

Later, while trying to remember exactly what I was doing at 5:40 p.m. that Friday afternoon, it came to me. I was in a shop admiring two sand dollars displayed in a box frame. The artist had carefully broken them both open, removed the ten white vertebrae that look like tiny doves and glued them in a flight formation on the mat above the dollars so they appeared to be rising out of the openings.

Eleven souls ascending to heaven, or nine souls escaping death through a crack between two train cars? In retrospect, I believe it represented both.